CHITRA BANERJEE DIVAKURNI'S MANIFESTO: A STUDY OF THEMES AND MOTIFS

PRIYANKA SINGLA

Made with ♥ on the Notion Press Platform

www.notionpress.com

TO MY MOTHER MRS. SHAMA SINGLA

Contents

Preface

It is my honor to present this book on some cultural and social concepts in Chitra Banerjee Divakaruni's works. Divakaruni, an award-winning author, is known for her heart- warming and meaningful stories that highlight the diversity and complexity of the Indian-American experience. Her writing touches on a range of themes such as identity, immigration, family dynamics, love, and loss. This book is an attempt to analyze and discuss some of the cultural and social concepts that are embedded in Divakaruni's works. The book is aimed at anyone who is interested in understanding the nuances of Indian culture and society, and how they intersect with the experiences of the Indian diaspora in America. Specifically, the book targets scholars, students, and enthusiasts of literature and cultural studies. The book begins with an introduction that provides a brief overview of Divakaruni's life and works. The succeeding chapters delve into specific cultural and social concepts that are integral to Divakaruni's literary universe. The chapters are organized thematically and each one analyzes a different concept such as family, gender, patriarchy, tradition, and identity. One of the strengths of this book is its reliance on a range of literary theories and interdisciplinary approaches such as postcolonial theory, feminist theory, and psychoanalytic theory. These approaches offer compelling insights into the ways in which Divakaruni's works engage with complex cultural and social realities. I hope that this book will provide readers with a deeper appreciation of Divakaruni's works and contribute to ongoing conversations about culture, identity, and representation in literature.

PRIYANKA SINGLA
ASSOCIATE PROF. OF ENGLISH
GOVERNMENT COLLEGE FOR WOMEN, HISAR.

Acknowledgements

This work is the sweet fruit of endless hours of hard labour which were put into it and which wouldn't at all have been possible without the constant support and encouragement of my mother Mrs. Shama Singla. I am eternally grateful to my teachers who shaped me into the student that I am today. Special thanks to Mr. Naib Singh, Associate Prof. of Commerce, GC, Ambala Cantt. for his constant guidance and support. Last but not least, I would like to acknowledge all my colleagues of the Department of English, GCW, Hisar, who were always available with their valuable inputs and suggestions.

Author's Bio

Priyanka Singla is an Associate Prof. of English who is currently posted at Government College for Women, Hisar. She has teaching experience of more than 16 years, and has more than 10 years experience of teaching PG classes as well. She has done her Ph.D. on the topic "Post Colonial Concerns in Bapsi Sidhwa's *Ice- Candy- Man* and *An American Brat* and Rohinton Mistry's *A Fine Balance* and *Family Matters*". Her areas of interest include- Post Colonialism, Queer Theory, Feminism, Cultural Theory, etc. She has attended and presented papers in many National and International Seminars and Conferences. She has, to her credit, more than 20 publications in various UGC Care and Peer Reviewed International Journals. She has also published three edited volumes and has authored one book titled "Post Colonial Concerns in Chitra Banerjee Divakurni's Works" as well. She is an avid reader and is ever ready to venture into new vistas of various new concepts and researches which appear on the literary plane of English Literature.

CHAPTER ONE

INTRODUCTION

Chitra Banerjee Divakaruni is a contemporary Indian writer of fiction, poetry, and essays in English. She is an award-winning author whose novels have gained international recognition and acclaim. Born in Kolkata, India, in 1956, Divakaruni moved to the United States in 1976 to pursue her graduate studies. She has since established herself as an internationally recognized author of novels, short stories, poetry, and essays. Her works have garnered numerous awards and accolades, including the American Book Award, the Pushcart Prize, and the Light of India Award. Additionally, her books have been translated into many languages and are widely read worldwide. Divakaruni is an important writer in contemporary Indian Writing in English for several reasons. Firstly, she has contributed significantly to the representation of Indian culture and identity in literature. Divakaruni's novels, such as *The Palace of Illusions, Sister of My Heart,* and *The Mistress of Spices,* provide insights into the lives of Indian women, their struggles, and their triumphs. Her works also explore themes of familial relationships, love, loss, and identity, among others. Divakaruni's representation of Indian culture and identity is both authentic and sensitive, thereby providing readers with a deeper understanding of the complexities of Indian society. Secondly, Divakaruni's unique literary style and voice make her an important writer of Indian Writing in English. Her prose is lyrical and poetic, with vivid imagery and metaphors that transport readers to the worlds she creates. Her writing is also marked by a deep sense of empathy and compassion towards her characters, which enables readers to connect emotionally with them. Divakaruni's use of magical realism, mythology, and symbolism is another hallmark of her literary style, which infuses her works with a sense of the otherworldly. Thirdly, Divakaruni's contribution to the field of literature is significant in terms of its impact on Indian Writing in English. She is part of a generation of writers who have redefined the contours of Indian literature, breaking away from the traditional canon of postcolonial writing. Divakaruni's works challenge existing norms, open up new forms of representation, and explore new perspectives on India, its culture, and its people. Her works provide insights into the lives of Indian women, their struggles, and their triumphs. Her unique literary style, marked by lyrical prose, magical realism, and symbolism, has captivated readers worldwide. Divakaruni belongs to a generation of writers who have redefined Indian literature, and her work challenges existing norms and offers new perspectives on Indian society and culture. Therefore, it is essential to recognize Divakaruni's contribution to the field of literature and appreciate her significance as a modern writer of Indian Writing in English.

Divakurni is one of the most celebrated writers of Indian origin in the contemporary world. Her works explore themes of identity, migration, gender and diaspora, and often draw heavily on myth and folklore. Her use of myth in her fiction highlights the importance of understanding the significance of traditional narratives in contemporary times. Myth serves as a bridge between the present and the past, connecting characters and events across time, space and culture. In Divakurni's novels, myths are retold, re-imagined, and deconstructed to explore their relevance to the present. Myths, as recurring motifs, play an essential role in establishing themes in Divakurni's novels. For instance, the *Mahabharata* is the central myth in *The Palace of Illusions,* which presents an alternate telling of the epic through the voice of Draupadi. The novel reinterprets the mythic narrative by giving voice to the women characters, transgressing the patriarchal norms of the original text. Similarly, in *The Mistress of Spices*, mythic folklores and fables are used to convey the transformative powers of spices. Tilo, the protagonist, uses her ability to communicate with spices to help her clientele find solace and healing. The motif of spices as potent sources of transformation is an extension of the traditional beliefs in the mystical properties of herbs and spices. Divakurni's use of myth in *Sister of My Heart,* on the other hand, is primarily a means of invoking the past lives of the protagonist's ancestors. Anju and Sudha, the two protagonists, must sift through myth and legend to uncover the truth about their family's past, unravelling the mysteries that have haunted the women for generations. Divakurni's work showcases how mythic narratives can offer insights into universal themes such as family, love, sacrifice, and belonging. Her portrayal of myths has an overarching message about the power of traditional narratives to inform and enrich contemporary culture. These fictional works demonstrate that myths can play significant roles in defining individual identities and in shaping cultural heritage. Divakurni's fiction is a testament to the enduring relevance of the mythic tradition and to its potential to contribute to the creation of a more complex and nuanced understanding of the world.

Divakurni's fiction frequently features female protagonists who challenge the patriarchal norms and expectations that govern their lives. One of the recurring themes in her novels is the representation of women who participate in political contexts, which this paper will focus on. In Divakurni's novels, female characters engage in various forms of political activities, ranging from community organizing, grassroots activism, to electoral politics. For instance, in her novel *Queen of Dreams*, the protagonist Rakhi participates in political campaigns as a campaign manager, helping a progressive candidate challenge a conservative incumbent. Similarly, in *The Mistress of Spices* and *Sister of My Heart,* the female protagonists use their leadership skills and political savvy to mobilize their communities and advocate for social justice. Divakurni's works challenge gender stereotypes about women's roles in politics. In many societies and cultures, women are often marginalized in political spheres and are expected to conform to traditional gender roles. However, Divakurni's female characters break free from these constraints and assert their agency as capable and effective leaders. They demonstrate that women can be political actors and agents of change, and that traditional gender roles and expectations should not limit their aspirations and potential. The portrayal of women in political contexts in Chitra Banerjee Divakurni's fiction highlights the complexities and challenges faced by women who aspire to be political leaders. It also underscores the importance of representation and visibility of women in positions of power and authority, not only in politics but in all spheres of life. Divakurni's works provide a powerful message to young women that they can aspire to be leaders and agents of change, and that they too can make a difference in their communities and beyond.

In her fiction, Divakurni explores the challenges of being a woman in a cultural context that often values traditional gender roles and norms. In *The Mistress of Spices*, Divakurni tells the story of Tilo, an Indian woman who can communicate with spices and uses her powers to help others. Through Tilo's experiences, Divakurni highlights the tension that can arise when women attempt to assert their independence in a traditional cultural context. Tilo yearns for love and connection, but is constrained by societal expectations that dictate how women should behave. Ultimately, Tilo's desire for autonomy leads her to reject the conventional path of marriage and family and embrace a life devoted to her craft. *The Palace of Illusions* is a retelling of the Indian epic, *The Mahabharata*, from the perspective of the female protagonist, Draupadi. In this novel, Divakurni reimagines Draupadi as a feminist icon who defies traditional gender roles and expectations. Draupadi is a complex character who is both empowered and constrained by her gender. She is a fierce warrior and leader, yet is ultimately defined by her relationships with men. Through Draupadi's story, Divakurni demonstrates the potential for women to challenge gender norms, while also depicting the difficulties they face in doing so. Divakurni's short story collection, *Arranged Marriage*, further explores the challenges faced by women in traditional cultures. The stories in this collection center on women negotiating marriages and relationships within their communities. Divakurni portrays women who must navigate the competing demands of family obligation and individual desire. In the title story, Arranged Marriage, Divakurni tells the story of an Indian woman who must choose between following her heart and obeying her family. Like many of Divakurni's characters, she is torn between societal expectations and personal fulfillment. Through her novels and stories, Divakurni has become known for her nuanced depictions of women navigating the complexities of cultural identity. Her characters grapple with the tension between societal expectations and individual desire, often in pursuit of some kind of personal fulfilment. Despite the challenges they face, Divakurni's women are not passive victims of their circumstances. Instead, they are complex and multifaceted individuals who are able to challenge traditional gender norms and expectations in their own ways. Through her fiction, Divakurni highlights the ways in which culture and gender intersect to shape women's experiences, while also showcasing the potential for resistance and autonomy.

Divakurni has made a significant contribution to the literary world with her piercing insight and precise descriptions of the lives of immigrant women in the diaspora. Her work is a testimony to the struggle, resilience, and determination of women who have dared to dream big and have the courage to transform their lives, despite social and cultural obstacles. Her work challenges traditional stereotypes of women, especially those from different cultural and social backgrounds. Her literature highlights the diverse struggles faced by women, the quest for personal identity, and the quest for power within patriarchy. Divakurni's works are a reflection of the evolving feminist ideas, which give voice to women's issues, acknowledging their diversity and the ways in which race, class, and gender intersect. The portrayal of women in her fiction is a reflection of the evolving feminist ideas, giving voice to women's challenges, acknowledging their diversity, and the ways in which race, class, and gender intersect. Her works challenge traditional stereotypes of women from different cultural and social backgrounds. Her characters face various issues, including immigrant experiences, acculturation, racism, and prejudices based on cultural and social differences. The portrayal of women in social contexts in Divakurni's fiction is a representation of the dynamic nature of women's lives. Her literature acknowledges the diverse struggles that women face in their quest for personal identity, status, and power within patriarchal societies. It highlights the importance of intersectional analysis in understanding the complexity of women's experiences, shaped by race, class, and gender.

Divakaruni's fiction addresses the theme of tradition versus modernity in the context of the Indian diaspora experience. Born in India and moved to the United States to pursue higher education in the mid-1970s, Divakaruni's writing often highlights the complexities and tensions that arise when traditional Indian values come into contact with contemporary Western values. Her characters are often caught in a struggle between the customs and practices of their homeland and the powerful allure of a more modern, American way of life. Divakaruni's characters often find themselves faced with difficult choices as they navigate the clash between tradition and modernity. Born and raised in India, her characters cling to the traditional cultural values, looking through a lens of cultural conservatism. They use them as the means to make sense of the world. Their significant beliefs are rooted and reinforced by the social and cultural environment they grow up in. At the same time, they must negotiate their relationships with an American society that embraces a more individualistic, freethinking, and progressive cultural standpoint. Divakaruni highlights the pressure faced by Indian young women in the US to embrace Western ways. In her short story collection, *Arranged Marriage*, Divakaruni tells the story of Sumita, a young Indian woman who comes to the US after an arranged marriage to an Indian-American man. Sumita is surprised and shocked to find that her husband has adopted a thoroughly

American lifestyle, and his family members are detached from Indian culture. She is expected to comply with American customs, which did not fall in line with her culture. Sumita finds herself at odds with the balancing act of trying to maintain her identity and fit in with her new community. A similar tension appears in Divakaruni's novel *Queen of Dreams*, in which the young protagonist, Rakhi struggles to reconcile her Indian roots with her growing sense of personal autonomy and self-assertion as an American citizen. Divakaruni's fiction is a reflection of the complexities and challenges of Indian diaspora experience. Her work points to the unsteady balance between continuity and transformation as immigrants negotiate different cultures and value systems. Since cultural identity is never static and continues to evolve, these stories that capture struggles occurring in the second-generation imagination will always hold relevance. By depicting the clash between tradition and modernity through her characters' stories, Divakaruni offers insights into the layered nature of the diasporic identity and the tensions that come with it.

Divakaruni's stories and novels are set in India, the United States, and sometimes a combination of both. She portrays the experiences of Indian women who navigate the conflicting demands of tradition and modernity, patriarchy and feminism, and migration and integration. She is a writer whose work centers on the experiences of Indian women. Her writing explores themes such as tradition, identity, gender, and race, placing her female characters in places where they face multiple struggles. Her stories often showcase the interplay of post-colonialism, feminism, and diaspora, which combine to examine South Asian women's unique experiences, particularly in terms of their own cultural heritage. Divakaruni's stories and novels are set primarily in India, but she also incorporates American settings into her work. Her writing often becomes an eloquent commentary on cultural differences, particularly those that arise from Indian traditions and move to American life. She takes us through a journey through Indian culture and eventually to America, where she expresses with eloquence the challenges of adaptation and integration faced by other migrants.

Divakaruni's writing focuses on the complexities and challenges of the Indian social milieu. India is noted for its distinct traditions, but as it becomes more globalized, these traditions have become subject to change. Indians living abroad continue to search for ways to keep them alive while still trying to integrate into their new country and society. The cultural context of the stories in Divakaruni's fiction is, therefore, much more complex than it appears at first glance. One central theme in her writing is identity. Her work focuses on how South Asian women navigate the intersection of identity markers such as gender, race, and culture, particularly in the face of patriarchal oppression. Many of Divakaruni's stories also highlight feminist themes, drawing attention to women's struggles with unequal power dynamics in relationships, including abusive relationships, and with the status quo in society. She tends to present her female characters as multi-dimensional and complex, often highlighting their strengths and vulnerabilities at the same time. Divakaruni's characters are notable for their depth, complexity, and relatability. She creates female characters that are at once relatable but also vivid representations of the complex social milieu in which they are set. Largely, her female characters often appear in her writing as the backbone and the foundation of their families, the anchor that holds everything together while facing insurmountable challenges with determination and resilience. Divakaruni's fiction masterfully intertwines Indian culture with the experiences of South Asian female characters living in India and the United States. Her stories delve into the complexities of the social milieu in which these female characters find themselves, and shine a light on the challenges intrinsic to navigating stringent traditions, cultural clashes, and patriarchal structures. In short, Divakaruni's work is significant for its intersectionality and representation of South Asian women's experiences in a changing world.

The portrayal of women in literature is a topic of great significance and relevance in today's society, where women's voices are being heard and their rights are being recognized. Divakaruni is celebrated for her insightful and poignant exploration of women's experiences. Her works have been described as culturally and socially relevant, contemporarily sensitive and suffused with feminist perspectives. Her depiction of characters is uniquely complex with complex cultural and historical roots. *The Mistress of Spices* tells the story of Tilo, a woman from India with supernatural powers, who runs a spice shop in Oakland, California. Tilo uses her powers to fulfil the needs of her customers, but she is forbidden from falling in love with any of them. Through Tilo's character, Divakaruni explores the themes of love, desire, sacrifice, and the tension between tradition and modernity. Tilo's struggles to navigate her cultural heritage and her own desires are emblematic of the challenges that many women face today. Her ability to form empathic connections with other women adds a further dimension, bringing emotional depth to the novel's themes.

The Palace of Illusions is a retelling of the Indian epic Mahabharata from the perspective of Draupadi, the wife of the five Pandava brothers. Through Draupadi's use of her voice, Divakaruni sheds light on the multiple injustices that women face in a deeply patriarchal society. Draupadi's intelligence and tenacity contribute to the resolution of the conflicts that arise, emphasizing the importance of women's agency in a male-dominated world. Her character also provides a valuable example of resilience in the face of oppression, serving as an inspirational figure for women who fight against injustice. Divakaruni's depiction of women in her fiction highlights the complexity of their experiences and the historical, social, and cultural factors that construct their identities. The Mistress of Spices and The Palace of Illusions both depict female characters who struggle against patriarchal societal norms and navigate their cultural heritage in their pursuit of personal fulfilment. Through the lenses of feminist and postcolonial theory, it becomes evident how Divakaruni's fiction contributes to the broader discourse around issues of gender, identity, and power, and serves as a vital recognition for a diverse array of feminine identities.

Cultural disparity refers to the differences in culture and lifestyles among diverse groups of people. This issue has been tackled in various literary works, and Chitra Banerjee Divakaruni's fiction is no exception. Her works delve into the lives of Indian women and their struggles with cultural displacement, identity, and the challenges of adapting to a new culture. One of the themes that Divakaruni explores is the cultural identity of Indian women who have migrated to the United States. In *Arranged Marriage,* the short story "The Bats," explores the clash of cultures between the protagonist's Indian heritage and the American culture. Preeti, the protagonist, is portrayed as coming from a traditional Indian background, but she finds it challenging to adjust to her new home in the United States. The differences in cultural values and traditions are evident in her relationship with her husband, who is more comfortable with American ways of doing things. Preeti feels lost and disoriented, and the disparity between the two cultures creates a gap that she struggles to bridge. Divakaruni's works also highlight the struggle of migrants trying to balance their traditional culture with the new culture that they find themselves in. The short story collection Arranged Marriage explores the experiences of Indian women who have migrated to the United States and their struggles with adapting to a new environment. In the title story, the protagonist Dipa, who grew up in the Indian culture, finds it difficult to cope with the American way of life. She feels isolated from her surroundings and longs for the traditional Indian ways of doing things. However, her husband, who is of Indian descent but grew up in America, is more comfortable with the western culture than the Indian one. The cultural disparity in Divakaruni's fiction is further explored in her novel *Sister of My Heart*. The novel examines the lives of two Indian girls, Anju and Sudha, who are cousins, and the challenges they encounter as they grow up. Sudha migrates to the United States, where she faces the pressure of adapting to a different culture while still holding onto her Indian identity. The novel vividly describes Sudha's struggles with her Indian heritage, her dreams, and her new reality. The stark cultural differences between the two worlds are shown when Sudha is forced to confront the challenges of her diminishing ties with her Indian culture and the distant relationship with her cousin.

Divakaruni has produced several works of fiction with themes that are relevant to a diverse range of readers. Her stories have been widely read in the United States and other parts of the world, and they are marked by various themes and motifs that help to create a multi-layered and complex vision of the Indian American experience. One of the most prominent themes in Divakaruni's work is the issue of cultural dislocation. Many of her characters -- like Anju and Sudha in Sister of My Heart – straddle two cultures and feel like they don't belong in either. This sense of dislocation is often accompanied by a search for identity, a theme that also features prominently in her work. Another key theme in Divakaruni's fiction is the role of women. In many of her stories, female characters are portrayed as strong, resilient, and intelligent but often find themselves trapped in oppressive cultural or social structures. She explores the ways in which women negotiate these structures, often highlighting their struggles and resilience. A third theme is the tension between tradition and modernity. Some characters – like Devi in *The Palace of Illusions* –struggle to reconcile their personal desires with the expectations of family and society. This theme is perhaps most clearly demonstrated by the generational conflicts that occur in her work, such as the struggles of immigrants trying to maintain their cultural heritage while adapting to a new world.

In addition to these themes, there are several motifs that are recurrent in Divakaruni's work. One of the most prominent is food. In many of her stories, food is used to represent comfort, identity, and family history. For example, in *One Amazing Thing*, characters wait together in a basement for rescue, sharing their personal stories in turn as a way to understand each other's differences and bond over commonality. What they decide to share reveal more crucial information than they intended to. In each of these stories, food plays a crucial role as the characters find comfort in the familiar tastes and smells of their shared cultural heritage. Another recurring motif is the use of legends and mythology. Divakaruni often draws on Indian myths and legends as a way to make sense of the contemporary world. In The Palace of Illusions, she reimagines the story of the Mahabharata from the point of view of Draupadi. The retelling of the old myth has provided an insight that makes the myth more relevant and relatable to modern readers. The themes and motifs attest to Divakaruni's literary talent in weaving a complex tapestry of the Indian-American experience. She excels in creating multidimensional characters with whom readers can empathize and identify. The exploration of themes such as cultural dislocation, the role of women, and the tension between tradition and modernity reflects a deep understanding of the complexities of the Indian-American identity. Her use of motifs such as food and mythology add beauty and depth to her storytelling, creating a richer and more vibrant tapestry for readers to engage with.

CHAPTER TWO

MAJOR THEMES

Chitra Banerjee Divakaruni is a significant figure in the world of Indian Writing in English, and her contributions as a woman writer have been invaluable. Her writing explores themes of cultural conflict, displacement, gender, and identity, making her a prominent voice for Indian women worldwide. This paper will examine the importance of Chitra Banerjee Divakaruni as a woman writer of Indian Writing in English and the significance of her work in contemporary literature. Her writing is unique in its ability to explore the experiences of women in contemporary society, particularly Indian women. Her female characters wade through the complexities of their identities as they navigate cross-cultural experiences. They represent and shed light on the experiences of women of color and have highlighted the unique ways women of color are likely to grapple with their gender and racial identities. For instance, in her novel, *The Mistress of Spices*, Divakaruni depicts the story of a woman of Indian descent who struggles to reconcile her heritage with her modern life in the US. The protagonist, Tilo, is a spice seller who uses the spices to help her customers, but must grapple with the consequences of overstepping the boundaries of her assumed role.

Divakaruni's writing is a testament to her deep affection for her Indian heritage. Her vivid depictions of Indian culture, values, and traditions give readers an intimate view of the complexities and richness of Indian life. Through her works, she aims to dispel stereotypes and present a more nuanced picture of Indian society. For instance, in her novel, *The Palace of Illusions*, Divakaruni retells the story of the Mahabharata from a feminist perspective, challenging the patriarchal norms that permeated the epic. In doing so, she highlights the cultural complexities within Indian society and exposes the internal tensions that often arise when traditional values clash with modern ones. She is an influential figure in Indian Writing in English and has playcd a significant role in shaping the literary landscape in India and worldwide. Her work has inspired other writers, especially women writers, to tell their stories and contribute to literary conversation. In *Sister of My Heart*, Divakaruni presents a remarkable and nuanced portrayal of the relationship between women that borrowed from a traditional tie but wrestled with the expectations of modern life. The plot highlights the complexities of motherhood, sisterhood, friendship, love, and duty, which had been rarely written about in Indian Literature in English. Divakaruni's position as a woman writer of Indian Writing in English excels with her ability to write about and represent Indian lives beyond stereotypes. Her writing provides a unique insight into the Indian community's cultural complexities and the challenges that women face daily. Through her writing, she has influenced and diversified the Indian literary world, establishing her position as a crucial voice of Indian women worldwide, challenging readers' mindsets and promoting empathy across borders.

Divakaruni's novels explore the tensions that arise from the intersection of traditional values and beliefs with modern ways of life. In this paper, we will analyze how Divakaruni depicts the theme of the clash between tradition and modernity in her novels and the impact of this conflict on the lives of her characters. The theme of the clash between tradition and modernity is a dominant motif in Divakaruni's works. Her novels often feature characters who are caught in the tension between the traditional ways of their cultural heritage and the contemporary ideals of the modern world. Through her storytelling, Divakaruni explores the challenges of reconciling the past and the present, and the complexities of navigating cultural identities in a rapidly changing world. For instance, in *Sister of My Heart*, the protagonists, Anju and Sudha, grow up in a traditional Indian household where arranged marriages and strict gender roles are the norm. However, as they come of age and are exposed to new ideas and experiences, they begin to question the traditions that have shaped their lives. The clash between tradition and modernity ultimately forces them to confront their own identities and the difficult choices they must make.

Similarly, in *The Palace of Illusions,* Divakaruni retells the story of the Mahabharata from the perspective of Draupadi, the epic's enigmatic heroine. The novel explores Draupadi's struggle to reconcile her traditional values and roles as a wife and mother with her desires for self-determination and independence. The clash between tradition and modernity has significant impacts on the lives of Divakaruni's characters.

The tension created by this conflict often leads to feelings of disorientation, confusion, and even trauma. Divakaruni's novels depict the complexities of navigating cultural identity, and the deep sense of loss that comes from the erosion of traditional values. The clash between tradition and modernity also impacts social relationships and community dynamics. In "Arranged Marriage," Divakaruni depicts the conflict between an Indian immigrant couple who have assimilated to Western culture and the husband's traditionalist mother who insists on upholding Indian customs. The resultant tension destroys the couple's relationship and fractures the entire family. Her novels depict the challenges of cultural identities in a rapidly changing world and the ways in which the struggle to reconcile tradition and modernity can profoundly impact individuals and communities. Through her characters' experiences, Divakaruni invites readers to consider the complexities of cultural identity and the importance of empathy in navigating the tensions between the past and the present.

In her works, one significant theme that surfaces repeatedly, is the patriarchal oppression of women. The patriarchal oppression of women is a common motif in Chitra Banerjee Divakaruni's works. Her female protagonists often find themselves struggling with their position within a culture that is dominated by men who expect women to be subservient, obedient, and to conform to traditional gender roles. For instance, in "Arranged Marriage," Divakaruni explores the theme of patriarchy through a series of short stories that depict the everyday struggles of Indian women living in the United States. The stories highlight the challenges of arranged marriages, domestic violence, and sexual exploitation that many women face within their communities. Similarly, in *The Mistress of Spices*, Divakaruni depicts the oppression of women in a patriarchal society by showing how Tilo, the protagonist of the novel, is forced to abide by the rigid societal norms and values on her path to self-discovery. Tilo's ability to break free from these oppressive expectations lies in her mastery of the spices, which provide her with the power to heal and transform the lives of women she encounters.

The patriarchal oppression of women has significant impacts on their lives and their ability to thrive. Divakaruni's works highlight these impacts, including limited opportunities for education, restricted access to jobs and employment, and susceptibility to domestic violence and sexual exploitation. This oppression can stifle women's creativity, limit their ability to make choices, and result in a narrow range of experiences that can lead to feelings of hopelessness, despair, and disempowerment. For instance, in *Sister of My Heart*, the protagonists Anju and Sudha, grow up in a society where their worth is determined by their success in achieving marriage and motherhood. Their aspirations and dreams are stifled by a society that places limits on their choices and forces them to endure the control and repression of men. Divakaruni's novels depict the struggles of women to break free from the constraints of patriarchal oppression and claim their own agency. Through her distinct storytelling, Divakaruni invites readers to understand the complexities of the female experience in a patriarchal society and the resilience and strength that women display in their fight for self-empowerment.

In her novels, she employs a rich and evocative language that brings her characters and their stories alive. Divakaruni's novels are rich in cultural references and are written in a language that reflects the unique cultural perspective of her characters. For example, in her novel *The Palace of Illusions*, Divakaruni uses a lyrical and poetic language to describe the cultural practices and traditions of ancient India. Her language is imbued with metaphors and symbols drawn from Hindu mythology, which adds a layer of depth and complexity to the text. Similarly, in *The Mistress of Spices*, Divakaruni uses a sensual and evocative language to describe the smells, textures, and tastes of the spices that Tilo, the protagonist of the novel, uses to heal and transform the lives of her customers. Through her use of language, Divakaruni portrays the cultural significance of spices in Indian cuisine and highlights their role in bringing together different cultural traditions.

Divakaruni's novels also explore the complexities of identity and the way language is used to express it. In *Queen of Dreams*, Divakaruni explores the relationship between a mother and daughter and the way they use language to express their emotions and connect with each other. The novel is written in a multi-lingual style, with the characters switching between English, Hindi, and Bengali, reflecting the cultural and linguistic diversity of their identities. In *Before We Visit the Goddess*, Divakaruni employs a similar multi-lingual style to portray the experiences of three generations of Indian-American women. The text is written in a mixture of English, Bengali, and Hindi, highlighting the way language is used to bridge the gap between different cultural and generational identities.

The use of language in Divakaruni's novels is significant in that it reflects the cultural and linguistic diversity of her characters and provides insights into the complex process of identity formation. Her novels challenge the standard English language conventions and present a different perspective, emphasizing the importance of multilingualism and cultural diversity. The use of figurative language and metaphors also reinforces the cultural significance of language and the way it shapes our understanding of the world around us. By employing a multi-lingual and figurative language, Divakaruni highlights the importance of cultural diversity and presents a unique perspective on identity formation. Through her novels, she invites readers to appreciate the beauty and richness of language and to recognize how it shapes our cultural identities.

Divakaruni's novels explore the intricate relationships between race, culture, and social identity, and the impact of these factors on individual lives. Through her works, she depicts how people of color experience marginalization and discrimination due to their race or ethnicity, and how these experiences play out in the larger social structures. For example, in her novel *Before We Visit the Goddess*, Divakaruni explores the experiences of three generations of women who identify as Indian-American. The novel portrays how these women navigate issues of race and identity in a culturally diverse yet racially divided society. Divakaruni highlights how economic and cultural marginalization can perpetuate cycles of poverty and limit social mobility, especially for people of color. In *The Mistress of Spices*, Divakaruni depicts the experiences of Tilo, a South Asian immigrant who struggles to find her place in American society. Through Tilo's interactions with other characters and the challenges she faces due to racial prejudices and biases, Divakaruni exposes how racism can become internalized, causing immigrants of color to struggle with their cultural identity and self-worth.

Divakaruni's novel, *Oleander Girl*, similarly portrays the struggles faced by an Indian-American woman in navigating her racial identity within American society. The novel provides insights into how individuals of color must confront biases and discrimination, while also grappling with their cultural heritage and individual identity. The theme of racial oppression in Divakaruni's novels is significant in that it provides a nuanced understanding of the systemic biases and prejudices that individuals of color face in society. It foregrounds how these biases work to restrict the opportunities of people of color, and presents the struggles faced by individuals in navigating their cultural identity, while confronting racism. The significance of this theme is further enhanced by the fact that

Divakaruni's novels expose the internalized racism that individuals of color may experience due to their social identity. This discussion is essential given that it enables readers to gain deeper insights into structures of oppression and its impact on the psyche of people of color. She provides nuanced insights into the struggles that individuals of color face in navigating their racial identity and confronting the biases and oppression that accompany it. Her works invite readers to reflect on their own biases and prejudices, and to commit themselves to fighting for social justice and equality.

Divakaruni explores themes of identity, culture, gender, and social justice in her novels. Her works highlight social injustices and the struggles of marginalized communities, and often challenge cultural norms and traditions. Divakaruni's novels often address the gender and social injustices that affect women's lives. In these works, she illustrates the oppression that women face in patriarchal societies, highlighting their marginalization and lack of autonomy. For example, in *The Palace of Illusions*, Divakaruni retells the Mahabharata from the perspective of Draupadi, who is forced into a marriage she does not want and is shamed and humiliated in public. This novel serves to expose the patriarchal norms and values that exist in the Indian society, and how they limit women's potential and agency. Similarly, in her novel *Sister of My Heart*, Divakaruni presents the plight of women in the Indian society, exploring the themes of gender hierarchy and power. In this novel, she portrays how the societal expectations that girls must marry and have children limit their potential and ability to achieve the goals they set for themselves. She brings into focus the daily struggles of women in patriarchal societies, from their struggle to assert their personal autonomy to make their own choices, to their struggles with fertility, love, and economic security.

Divakaruni's works also highlight the ways in which systemic structures of power and oppression impact people of color. In her novel, *Before We Visit the Goddess*, she explores the experiences of three generations of women, all of whom identify as Indian-American. Through the interaction of the characters with the larger social structures, she shows how economic and cultural marginalization can perpetuate the cycle of poverty and limit one's social mobility. By exploring the generational stories, she highlights the ways in which systemic oppression can be internalized, and how it can shape the lives and choices of individuals. In addition, in her novel *The Mistress of Spices*, Divakaruni examines issues of racism, immigration, and cultural identity. In this novel, she portrays the protagonist, Tilo, as a South Asian immigrant who struggles to navigate the complexities of her cultural identity, while encountering racism and discrimination in her American community. By exploring these struggles and conflicts, she highlights the impact of racism and discrimination on individual lives, and how it can limit the opportunities and achievements of people of color. The theme of social equality and justice in Divakaruni's novels is significant in that it exposes the biases and oppressive forces that manifest in social structures. She highlights how the intersectionality of identities can lead to systemic discrimination and marginalization. She brings into focus the struggles, challenges, and achievements of women and people of color, thereby providing insights into their experiences and vulnerabilities. Through Divakurni's novels, she highlights the social structures that create and maintain inequalities, and shows how marginalized communities navigate them. Her works provide insightful commentary on the intersections of identity and the complexity of struggles faced by marginalized communities. By shedding light on these issues, she invites the readers to reflect on their own attitudes and biases, thereby fostering a deeper understanding and a commitment to social justice.

In many of Divakaruni's novels, family relationships are central to the plot and character development. She portrays Indian families, in particular, as complex systems of interconnected relationships. These families are often marked by deep love and loyalty as well as tension and conflicts. In *Sister of My Heart,* Divakaruni explores the relationship between two cousins, Anju and Sudha. The novel dives into their closeness, the ups and downs of their relationship, and their unwavering support for each other, even during difficult times. Through their relationship, Divakaruni highlights the emotional complexities and shared experiences that bind families together. Divakaruni also explores the theme of friendship in her novels. Her characters often form close bonds with others outside their families, creating extended support networks. These friendships provide a sense of belonging and emotional support, often helping characters navigate difficult situations and personal growth.

In *One Amazing Thing,* Divakaruni portrays the relationship between nine strangers trapped in a building after a natural disaster. The novel shows the characters' individual stories, but it is their shared experience that binds them together. During their confinement, they come to rely on each other, share their stories, and develop a sense of camaraderie that transcends their individual differences. Divakaruni demonstrates how the common experiences that bind these characters together can lead to enduring friendships. She also portrays romantic relationships in her novels, highlighting the complexities and power dynamics within them. Her characters are often conflicted between their own desires and societal expectations, leading to tension and misunderstandings. In "Arranged Marriage," Divakaruni explores the experiences of women who enter arranged marriages. Through various short stories, she shows the complexities of these relationships, highlighting how cultural expectations often shape them. She produces tales of women who defy expectations in their relationships, highlighting the power of individual will alongside culturally driven social forces, and gives insight into the nature of these relationships and how they can both restrict and liberate women.

The theme of interpersonal relationships in Divakaruni's novels is significant as it underscores our need for social connection and support. Her works show how outside relationships, whether they are with family or friends and romantic partners, can influence and shape our perceptions, beliefs, and actions. Relationships in Divakaruni's novels give readers insight into the emotional complexities of everyday interactions and how they can affect our sense of identity and self-worth. Furthermore, interpersonal relationships in Divakaruni's novels contribute to a broader understanding of the nature of human bonds. She portrays relationships as sources of both tension and comfort, emphasizing our capacity to love, support, and empathize with one another despite our differences. Divakaruni's novels highlights the complexity of human bonds and their significance in shaping our identities and sense of self-worth. Divakaruni portrays family, friendship, and romantic relationships as sources of both tension and comfort, emphasizing the importance of social support and connection in our lives. Th

One of the recurring themes in Divakaruni's works is the exploration of marginalization experienced by individuals in society. Her novels highlight how individuals can be marginalized based on various aspects of their identity, including race, ethnicity, gender, and social class. Her novels provide a nuanced exploration of the experiences of marginalized individuals in society. Her characters often face discrimination and prejudice due to their race, ethnicity, gender, or social class. These characters struggle to find their place in a society that marginalizes them and often face alienation and isolation. Divakaruni's novels highlight the complex social structures that lead to marginalization and their impact on individuals' lives. In her novel, *The Mistress of Spices*, Divakaruni explores the experiences of Tilo, an Indian-American woman who is also a spice seller and healer. Tilo is marginalized in both Indian and American societies, as she is not fully accepted by either culture. Her position as a woman of color, an immigrant, and a healer makes her an outsider in the societies she inhabits. Divakaruni's novel highlights the complexities of navigating multiple identities and the challenges of being marginalized in society.

Similarly, in *Before We Visit the Goddess*, Divakaruni examines the experiences of three generations of women in a family who face marginalization due to their social class and gender. The novel spans different time periods and explores the women's lives as they navigate social expectations and systemic barriers to achieve their dreams. Divakaruni's novel underscores how social structures can lead to marginalization and how individuals navigate these structures to find their place in society. The theme of marginalization in Divakaruni's novels is significant as it highlights the complex ways in which individuals experience discrimination and prejudice in society. Her novels offer a nuanced insight into the experiences of marginalized individuals and the impact that marginalization can have on their lives, highlighting the need for social change to address these injustices. Furthermore, the significance of the theme of marginalization lies in its ability to provide individuals who are marginalized with a voice and representation, enabling them to recognize their experiences and challenges in society. Through her works, Divakaruni offers a platform for the voices of marginalized individuals to be heard, empowering them to challenge systemic barriers and participate fully in society. Banerjee Divakaruni's novels highlight the theme of marginalization and its impact on individuals' lives. Her works explore the experiences of marginalized individuals due to their race, ethnicity, gender, or social class, highlighting the complexities of navigating social structures that perpetuate marginalization. The theme of marginalization in Divakaruni's novels underscores the need for social change and the empowerment of individuals to challenge systemic barriers and participate fully in society. Through her works, Divakaruni provides a voice and representation for marginalized individuals, empowering them to recognize their experiences and work towards greater social equity and justice.

One of the prominent themes in Divakaruni's works is the exploration of gender roles and the challenges and complexities faced by women in patriarchal societies. Divakaruni's novels provide a powerful critique of gender expectations and norms in South Asian culture and offer a nuanced examination of the experiences of women in those societies. Her novels, particularly those set in South Asia, delve into the complexities of gender roles and expectations, highlighting the prejudices and discriminations that women face in patriarchal societies. Her female characters are often portrayed as struggling to assert their agency and navigate a male-dominated world that seeks to limit their opportunities and choices. Divakaruni's novels offer a nuanced exploration of the challenges faced by women and provide a platform for women's voices to be heard. In her novel, *The Palace of Illusions*, Divakaruni explores the experiences of the female character Draupadi, who is often regarded as a symbol of feminine power and strength in Hindu myth. Draupadi's story is one of resilience, as she must navigate the male-dominated world of Mahabharata and assert her agency in a society that is hostile to women's voices. Through Draupadi's story, Divakaruni highlights the limitations imposed on women in a patriarchal society and the need to challenge gender expectations and norms.

Similarly, in *Sister of My Heart*, Divakaruni examines the lives of two young women, Anju and Sudha, who are bound by a deep and enduring friendship. The novel explores the challenges faced by women concerning gender expectations and roles in Indian society, including arranged marriage, domestic violence, and gender-based discrimination. Divakaruni's novel subverts traditional gender roles, depicting women as agents of their lives and capable of challenging societal norms. The significance of the theme of gender roles in Divakaruni's novels lies in its ability to challenge the dominant patriarchal discourse in South Asian culture. By offering a nuanced portrayal of women's experiences, Divakaruni exposes the limitations and challenges faced by women and challenges the reader to question the gender expectations and roles imposed by society. The relevance of this theme extends beyond South Asia to other cultures as well, where women are still struggling to assert their agency and challenge societal norms. Furthermore, the importance of the theme of gender roles lies in its ability to provide women with a voice and agency, offering them a platform to share their stories and experiences. Divakaruni's novels highlight the importance of women's voices and perspectives and offer a powerful critique of patriarchy, gender discrimination, and gender-based violence. Her works highlight the limitations and challenges faced by women and offer a nuanced exploration of gender-based discrimination and violence. Divakaruni's novels subvert traditional gender roles and depict women as agents of their lives, challenging societal norms and expectations. The theme of gender roles in Divakaruni's novels thus acquires significant importance as it offers women a voice and agency, empowering them to challenge the status quo and work towards a more equitable and just society.

One of the recurring themes in Divakaruni's works is the exploration of cultural traditions and their significance in shaping the characters' lives. Divakaruni's novels offer a unique perspective on the customs and practices of South Asia while highlighting the importance of maintaining cultural traditions in an ever-changing modern world. In her novels, cultural traditions are ever-present, and they play a significant role in shaping the characters' lives. These traditions define the characters' values, beliefs, and behaviors, and they often provide a sense of continuity and stability in their lives. The characters are deeply connected to their cultural heritage, and they struggle to reconcile their traditional beliefs with the modern world. In the novel *The Palace of Illusions*, Divakaruni explores the cultural traditions of ancient India through the retelling of the *Mahabharata* from the perspective of Draupadi, the wife of the five Pandavas. The novel provides a unique perspective on the customs, rituals, and beliefs of ancient India, while also highlighting the characters' struggles to navigate the shifting cultural landscape. Divakaruni beautifully weaves together the themes of tradition and modernity, demonstrating the complex relationship between the two.

In another novel, *Sister of My Heart*, Divakaruni explores the cultural traditions of South India. The novel tells the story of two cousins, Anju and Sudha, who grew up in different worlds but remain deeply connected by their shared heritage. The novel delves into various cultural practices, such as arranged marriages, gender roles, and the importance of family. Through the characters' experiences, Divakaruni highlights the importance of maintaining cultural traditions while also acknowledging the need for change and evolution. Similarly, in *The Mistress of Spices*, Divakaruni explores the cultural traditions of India through the character of Tilo, a young woman who possesses mystical powers and uses them to help those in need. The novel delves into the cultural significance of spices in ancient

India and their role in healing, love, and magic. Through Tilo's journey, Divakaruni highlights the importance of preserving cultural traditions while adapting them to the changing world. Her works provide a unique perspective on the customs and practices of South Asia while encouraging readers to appreciate and embrace cultural diversity. The exploration of cultural traditions in her works emphasizes the importance of preserving heritage while adapting to the changing world. Divakaruni's novels offer a fascinating and insightful look into South Asian culture, its customs, and its timelessness.

Divakaruni explores numerous critical themes in her works. One of the most important of these themes is cultural disparity. Cultural disparity refers to the divide between different cultures, particularly if they demand different expectations and values from the people living within them. In her novels, Divakaruni closely examines cultural disparity, particularly in the context of South Asian women who are confronted with multifaceted identities. Her novels explore the cultural disparity that exist between various cultures through the viewpoints of South Asian women. She delicately reveals the differences between the cultures forced upon women, particularly those who migrate from South Asia to America. The cultural disparities lead these women to have a disjointed identity, and Divakaruni explores this conflict through her characters who face it in real life. In her novel, *Before We Visit the Goddess*, Divakaruni illuminates how the cultural disparities between South Asia and America impact three generations of women. The novel explores how the Indian culture, as passed down from generation to generation, conflict with American culture, particularly for the younger generation. The novel depicts how the younger generation feels disconnected from their cultural heritage, and the older generation feels alienated from American culture, leading to a rift between them.

Likewise, in *The Mistress of Spices*, the cultural disparities between the Hindu and the American cultures force Tilo (the protagonist) to balance her inherent identities while confronting the contradictions between the two cultures. Tilo's expectations, her power, and her limitations as a woman within the Indian and American societies play a major role in her identity formation, leading to a culturally disparate existence. Furthermore, Divakaruni's novel, Arranged Marriage, explores the cultural disparities faced by South Asian women who are expected to conform to traditions that often limit their potential in society. The novel highlights how cultural disparities lead to conflicts between families, as they try to navigate their way through the varying expectations placed upon them. The young women in these families must reconcile the opposing cultural expectations while maintaining their individual identities. Divakaruni's novels vividly illustrate the numerous cultural disparities that exist between different cultures, particularly for South Asian women who are living a conflicted life in America. In exploring these disparities, Divakaruni reveals the varying cultural values and expectations that impact the identity formation of women from different cultures. These women must navigate these disparities and maintain their own identities in the face of cultural conflict. This theme highlights the importance of cultural awareness and understanding, and Divakaruni's novels offer a new perspective on the multiple cultural experiences of South Asian women. They allow readers to confront the challenges of cultural disparity and the need for cultural diversity and acceptance in modern society.

Divakaruni's characters frequently struggle with their individual and cultural identities. They wrestle with opposing expectations and societal norms that often limit their ability to fulfill their potential or purpose. In *Sister of My Heart*, for instance, Anju and Sudha confront the challenge of balancing their Indian heritage and American education. Anju feels unmoored and disconnected from both her past and current identity, while Sudha struggles to assert her independence from her arranged marriage. As such, they must navigate the expected roles prescribed to them within their cultural context and develop their individual identities. Similarly, in *Oleander Girl*, Korobi Roy confronts an existential crisis when she learns of her family's secrets, causing her to question her own identity. She grapples with the tension between her family's traditional values and her individual desires, particularly as she navigates the various patriarchal cultural expectations thrust upon her. Eventually, she must decide her identity as a woman, an Indian, a Bengali, and an American while doing what is best for her. The significance of these conflicts is particularly important when examining Divakaruni's novels. Her novels display the duality of identities and the search for their place in the world of South Asian women who may feel lost in multiple cultures' in-between spaces, thereby illuminating their internal struggles.

In Divakaruni's novels, we see a dynamic engagement with gender identity. This theme is evident in *The Palace of Illusions*, where Draupadi's gender identity and the expectations that accompany it become the primary focus of her struggles. As an empowered woman and formidable warrior,

Draupadi is frequently at odds with the patriarchal society surrounding her, which sees her as merely a wife or as having the responsibility to bear a male heir. In this novel, gender norms become a concern for Draupadi as she seeks to assert her independence in a world that seeks to limit her potential. Similarly, in *The Mistress of Spices*, Tilo must navigate the expectations placed on her from the mostly male leadership of the community, which often limits her abilities because of her gender. The inherent gender struggles, therefore, become intertwined and central to her search for identity and, consequently, her overall journey in the novel. The exploration of cultural identity is another, recurrent theme in Divakaruni's novels. In *Before We Visit the Goddess*, she examines the complexities of the Indian-American immigrant experience through three generations of women. Divakaruni highlights the challenges of maintaining cultural traditions while simultaneously acclimating to American society. As each of these generations tries to maintain its values, they find themselves struggling to negotiate individuality, particularly for the younger generation, who must decide their place within both cultures. Moreover, the tension between the East and the West is further explored in "Arranged Marriage", where the characters are challenged by the cultural traditions and societal expectations born out of their South Asian roots, often forcing them to confront their own preconceptions of what their individual identity should be.

The search for identity is a dominant theme in Divakaruni's novels, as the characters confront cultural and social constraints that inhibit their self-discovery. In *Sister of My Heart*, Anju and Sudha struggle to understand their identities within the context of their family's traditional Hindu culture. Anju is caught between her Indian heritage and American education, while Sudha yearns for independence and freedom from her arranged marriage. Similarly, in *One Amazing Thing*, a diverse group of strangers becomes trapped in an embassy after an earthquake, leading them to confront their past mistakes and uncertain futures. Through sharing personal stories, the characters reveal their search for identity in a world where cultural boundaries have become blurred. The struggles of women are another prominent theme in Divakaruni's novels. Her works tackle issues such as discrimination, oppression, and gender inequality. In *The Palace of Illusions*, Draupadi challenges the patriarchal society that defines her role as a wife and encourages her to embrace her identity as a warrior. She confronts gender-based discrimination and the male-centric portrayal of history as she navigates a society that tries to limit her power and choices.

In *The Mistress of Spices*, Tilo is forced to confront harsh realities in a world dominated by men. Despite being a skilled and insightful healer, she is relegated to running a spice shop and is subjected to harassment and discrimination from her male counterparts. Divakaruni portrays the struggles that women face in male-centric societies and provides insights into how women can overcome them. An exploration of cultural traditions is a significant theme in Divakaruni's novels. Her works often contrast the values and traditions of Indian culture with Western ideals, offering insights into the cultural clashes that shape the immigrant experience. In *Before We Visit the Goddess*, the novel explores the themes of family traditions and generational conflict. The story follows the lives of three generations of Indian women as they face the challenges of adapting to a new culture in America. The novel explores themes of identity, mother-daughter relationships, and the struggle to reconcile Indian traditions with modern American society. In "Arranged Marriage," the collection of short stories portrays the lives of South Asian women who confront the limitations of tradition and explore female empowerment. Divakaruni offers an insight into the complex relationship between tradition and modernity, as the characters grapple with the demands of family and expectations of society. She explores a range of themes that probe the challenges of the human experience. The search for identity, the struggles of women, and the exploration of cultural traditions offer insights into the complex nature of human nature, and the complexities of cultural identity. Divakaruni's works provide a glimpse into a world where cultures collide, and social norms are challenged, offering us insights into how to navigate the complexities of modern life. Her treatment of themes provides a depth of understanding and empathy that is both illuminating and inspiring.

CHAPTER THREE

PORTRAYAL OF WOMEN IN POLITICAL AND SOCIAL CONTEXTS

Women's empowerment and gender equality have been major challenges in various parts of the world, particularly in developing nations. Chitra Banerjee Divakaruni's novels depict the experiences of women who confront gender-oriented stereotypes and constraints in political and economic contexts. In *The Palace of Illusions*, Draupadi is portrayed as someone with intelligence, courage, and strength. However, her gender restricts her from actively participating in the political system. She is excluded from taking leadership roles, and her opinions are undervalued. Similarly, in *Before We Visit the Goddess*, Sabitri's political influence is limited by her gender and social status. Despite her intelligence and ambition, she experiences discrimination and oppression. In *Sister of My Heart*, Anju's prospects for political power are also diminished due to gender and caste inequalities. Her father prioritizes her marriage over her education and political aspirations, resulting in Anju's exclusion from political participation. Sudha's political power is curtailed by her gender and marital status. When her husband abandons her, Sudha is left without any political backing or resources. In *The Forest of Enchantments*, myths embrace gender stereotypes portraying women as inactive and submissive. Due to patriarchal norms, Sita is excluded from decision-making roles, and her opinions go unheard. In *The Mistress of Spices*, Tilo's economic power is limited by gender stereotypes portraying women as passive and subservient. She is given permission to operate a spice shop, which is deemed a woman's responsibility, while men control other businesses and industries. Tilo faces discrimination and exploitation from her male counterparts, resulting in restricted access to economic power.

Similarly, in *Before We Visit the Goddess*, Sabitri's economic power is limited by her gender and social status. She is forced to work in low-paying jobs, which barely help her fulfil her basic needs. Sabitri's lack of economic resources reduces her ability to support herself and her family, leaving her exposed to exploitation and discrimination from employers. In *The Palace of Illusions*, Draupadi's economic power is restricted by her gender and married status. She is dependent on her husband for financial support, making her vulnerable to exploitation and discrimination. Draupadi's economic dependency limits her choices and reduces her opportunities. The portrayal of gender stereotypes in political and economic contexts is critical since it exposes the ways in which gender discrimination limits women's access to resources and power. It highlights the need for gender equality and equal access to decision-making and leadership positions. Moreover, it promotes awareness of social norms and values that reinforce gender stereotypes and biases. Portraying these gender limitations and difficulties also inspires women to pursue political and economic power despite societal barriers and challenges. It encourages women not to settle for deficient representation; instead, it offers inspiration and evidence that women can own roles that have not traditionally been associated with them. Divakurni illustrates the challenges that women confront in political and economic contexts due to gender stereotypes. These stereotypes reduce women's access to power and resources while reinforcing patriarchal norms and biases. By portraying these limitations and hardships, Divakaruni's novels encourage critical reflection on gender stereotypes and biases and encourage women to pursue political and economic power.

In *The Palace of Illusions*, Draupadi is portrayed as an intelligent and strong woman, but her gender limits her participation in the political system. She is excluded from decision-making and leadership roles, and her opinions and desires are ignored. Similarly, in *Before We Visit the Goddess*, Sabitri's political power is limited by her gender and socioeconomic status. Despite her intelligence, hard work, and ambition, she faces discrimination and exclusion from political positions. In *Sister of My Heart*, Anju's political power is limited by gender and caste discrimination. Her father prioritizes her marriage over her education and career prospects, limiting her access to political power. Sudha's political power is limited by her gender and marital status. Her husband abandons her, leaving her with no political support or resources. In *The Forest of Enchantments*, Sita's political power is limited by gender stereotypes that view women as passive and submissive. She is excluded from decision-making, and her opinions and desires are suppressed by patriarchal norms.

In *The Mistress of Spices*, Tilo's economic power is limited by gender stereotypes that see women as passive and subservient. She is only allowed to own a spice shop, which is considered a "woman's job," while men control other businesses and industries. She faces discrimination and exploitation from male counterparts, limiting her access to economic power. In *Before We Visit the Goddess*, Sabitri's economic power is limited by her gender and socioeconomic status. She is forced to take up low-paying jobs, leaving her struggling to make ends meet. Her lack of economic resources limits her ability to help herself and her family, and she faces discrimination and exploitation from employers. In *The Palace of Illusions*, Draupadi's economic power is limited by her gender and marital status. She is dependent on her husband for financial support, leaving her vulnerable to exploitation and discrimination. Her lack of economic independence limits her choices and opportunities. The portrayal of gender stereotypes in political and economic contexts is significant because it exposes the ways in which gender discrimination limits women's access to power and resources. It highlights the need for gender equality and equal access to decision-making and leadership roles. It also encourages critical reflection on social norms and values that reinforce gender stereotypes and biases. These stereotypes limit women's access to power and resources and reinforce patriarchal norms and biases. By portraying these limitations and challenges, Divakaruni's novels encourage critical reflection on gender stereotypes and biases and inspire women to pursue political and economic power.

In *The Palace of Illusions*, Draupadi's lack of economic independence limits her choices and exposes her to economic vulnerability. Without the ability to earn her own income, she is dependent on her husband and faces discrimination and exploitation. Similarly, in *Before We Visit the Goddess*, Sabitri's low-paying job leaves her struggling to make ends meet, and her lack of economic resources limits her ability to help her family. Economic marginalization forces Sabitri to make difficult choices, and she struggles to provide for herself and her family. In *Sister of My Heart*, Anju and Sudha's economic conditions intersect with other issues, such as gender and caste discrimination. Anju's father prioritizes her marriage over her education and professional growth, and Sudha's husband abandons her, leaving her with no financial support. Both women are economically disempowered, limiting their access to education, employment, and other opportunities. Their lack of economic independence forces them to rely on, and be vulnerable to, the decisions of others. In *The Mistress of Spices*, Tilo's economic empowerment is limited by patriarchal norms that view women's economic independence as a threat to traditional gender roles. Tilo's magic, which could potentially make her financially independent, is feared and suppressed by her male counterparts. Her lack of economic empowerment leaves her vulnerable to exploitation and discrimination, and her resources are limited to her spice shop. Women's economic empowerment is crucial for achieving gender equality and social justice. It allows women to exercise greater control over their lives, make choices that reflect their values and goals, and challenge patriarchal norms and biases. Economic empowerment enables women to access education, employment, and financial resources, fostering their personal, social, and professional growth. Women's economic empowerment also promotes inclusivity and social justice. It enables women from all backgrounds to overcome economic barriers that prevent them from realizing their full potential and contributes to breaking the cycle of intergenerational poverty and gender inequality. Economic empowerment also challenges gender-based discrimination and engenders a fairer, more just society where women have equal economic opportunities. Divakaruni's novels illustrate the need for women's economic empowerment in achieving gender equality and social justice. These novels inspire women to pursue economic empowerment, and urge society to recognize the importance of women's economic empowerment in promoting gender equality and social justice.

In *The Palace of Illusions*, Draupadi's lack of education limits her opportunities to contribute to society and live an independent life. Despite her intelligence and curiosity, her access to knowledge is restricted because of her gender. Similarly, in *Before We Visit the Goddess*, Sabitri is denied access to education because her family believes women do not need an education. Her lack of education limits her job prospects and financial opportunities, making her economically vulnerable. In *Sister of My Heart*, Anju's ambition to pursue higher education is thwarted by patriarchal norms that prioritize marriage over personal development. Her cousin Sudha, who marries early to secure her financial future, experiences financial insecurity when her husband abandons her. Their lack of financial independence limits their ability to make choices and control their lives.

In *The Mistress of Spices*, Tilo's extraordinary powers are held back by the gendered expectations placed on women. Her access to education and professional opportunities is limited, and her magical powers are seen as a threat rather than an asset. The novel emphasizes the importance of equal access to resources for women's economic, social, and personal growth. Equal access to resources is essential for promoting gender equality, and Divakaruni's novels emphasize this point. When women have equal access to education, employment, and financial resources, they can challenge patriarchal norms and biases. Access to resources facilitates economic stability, personal growth, and independence, enabling women to control their lives and make choices that are not determined by gender roles. Equal access to resources also promotes inclusivity and social justice. It enables women from all backgrounds, including marginalized communities, to overcome economic, social, and political barriers that prevent them from realizing their full potential. It also helps to break the cycle of intergenerational poverty and gender inequality, establishing a fairer and more just society. By highlighting the significance of equal access to resources, Divakaruni's novels inspire and empower women to take control of their lives and challenge gender-based discrimination.

In *The Palace of Illusions*, Draupadi's resistance against her oppressive circumstances is one of the key elements of the story. Despite her reliance on her husbands, she takes charge of her own life when it comes to decision-making. For example, when she is insulted in court, she decides to seek justice and defend herself. She also refuses to be treated like a trophy and asserts herself when she is to be shared among the brothers as a wife. Such actions demonstrate her resistance against patriarchal norms. In *Sister of My Heart*, the protagonist, Anju, rebels against the expectation that she must marry to secure her financial future. She breaks off an arranged marriage, despite social pressure and familial obligations, to pursue her education and a career. Similarly, her cousin Sudha, who is forced into an unhappy marriage for financial stability, ultimately decides to leave her husband and find a job to support herself and her child. Their resistance, although different, is essential in asserting their agency in the face of patriarchal oppression. In Before We Visit the Goddess, Sabitri's resistance is subtler, but equally important. Despite being denied an education, she becomes a successful businesswoman and supports her daughter's education. Her efforts to build a life for herself and her family demonstrate her determination to break free from economic dependence.

In *The Mistress of Spices*, the protagonist Tilo uses her magical powers to empower women who visit her store. She helps women find jobs and become financially independent, indicating resistance against the patriarchal expectation that women must rely on men for financial stability. Women's resistance in Divakaruni's novels is significant because it shows that women are not passive victims of patriarchal oppression; they have the agency to take control of their lives and resist oppressive structures. It demonstrates the importance of fighting against the expectation that women must rely on men for their financial well-being. Women's resistance in economic contexts is also crucial in breaking the cycle of poverty and inequality that patriarchal norms perpetuate. Moreover, the representation of women's resistance in Divakaruni's works is empowering for women who may be facing similar circumstances. It gives them the courage to stand up against oppressive systems and assert their agency. In addition, it helps to challenge societal norms and promotes gender equality by showing that women can be self-sufficient and independent. It demonstrates that women are not mere victims of patriarchal oppression and have the power to take control of their lives. The representation of women's resistance in Divakaruni's works is empowering for women and helps to challenge societal norms that perpetuate gender discrimination.

In *The Palace of Illusions*, Draupadi is a victim of patriarchal oppression when she is forced to marry the five Pandava brothers. Later, when the brothers lose their kingdom, they become exiles, taking Draupadi with them. She finds it difficult to adjust to the harsh realities of exile and the economic struggles associated with it. The male-dominated society refuses to give her opportunities to work and earn a livelihood, and she is forced to rely on her husbands. Similarly, in *Sister of My Heart*, Anju and Sudha face patriarchal oppression while growing up in a conservative Indian society. They are not allowed to work and earn money for fear of losing their chastity. This lack of economic independence severely limits their choices in life and even the jobs they can take up in the future. Moreover, their societal and familial expectations force them to seek marriage as the only solution to their economic problems. In *Before We Visit the Goddess*, Sabitri is a victim of gender discrimination when her father refuses to educate her because she is a woman. Later, she is forced to work as a maid to pay for her daughter's education. Even though she is a resourceful woman who can earn money, she is held back by societal expectations that dictate that a woman's place is in the home, not in the workforce.

In *The Mistress of Spices*, Tilo is oppressed by her male-dominated society, which refuses to allow her to use her spice powers to help others. Instead, she is forced to work in a spice store to make ends meet. Her economic struggles are compounded by the patriarchal norms that dictate she must marry and have children. Her attempts to break free from these conventions and use her powers to help people are met with contempt. The patriarchal oppression that women face in Divakaruni's novels has a profound impact on their lives. Women are denied the opportunity to work and reach their full potential. They are forced to rely on men for financial support and are thus denied control over their own lives. The gender gap in income and employment opportunities reinforces societal norms that perpetuate gender discrimination and contributes to women's economic struggles. Moreover, patriarchal oppression in economic contexts has a ripple effect throughout society. Women's lack of economic independence limits their ability to invest in themselves and their communities, perpetuating the cycle of poverty and inequality. The societal norms that deny women the opportunity to work and earn a livelihood contribute to gender inequality, poverty and the cycle of oppression. Patriarchal oppression has a profound impact on women's lives, limiting their choices and robbing them of the opportunity to reach their full potential. Divakaruni's works are an urgent reminder of the need for systemic change to break free from patriarchal norms, give women greater economic independence, and build a more equitable society.

In *The Palace of Illusions*, Divakaruni depicts the economic struggle of Draupadi, the protagonist, who is forced to endure years of exile with her husbands, losing her status and wealth. Her forced relocation from the palace to the forest and the subsequent hardships she faced represents the economic struggle of women at that time. In *Sister of My Heart*, Divakaruni depicts the difficulties faced by Anju and Sudha in trying to raise their families in poverty. Their struggles to make ends meet and provide for themselves and their families are emblematic of the economic hardship experienced by women in India. The novel *Before We Visit the Goddess*, explores the lives of three generations of women, including Sabitri, who works as a maid to pay for her daughter's education, and Bela, who finds herself struggling to support her family after a divorce.

The short story *The Disappearance*, portrays the plight of an undocumented Indian immigrant faced with the challenges of surviving in the United States without legal papers or proper documentation. The main character's desperation to make ends meet and support her family represents the economic struggles of many immigrant women in the US. Economic independence is a crucial component of ensuring that women are able to make independent decisions and have control over their lives. It allows them to provide for themselves and their families and invest in their education and careers. Moreover, it empowers women to take charge of their own lives and break free from societal expectations and restrictions. Divakaruni's novels illustrate the importance of economic independence in allowing women to achieve their dreams and aspirations. The struggles that her characters are faced with highlight the obstacles that women in many societies still face today in trying to achieve self-sufficiency. The importance of economic independence in empowering women and giving them a voice to make independent decisions cannot be overstated. By shedding light on the economic struggles faced by women in her novels, Divakaruni urges readers to become more aware of the issues and barriers that impact women's economic independence and work towards creating a more equitable society.

Divakaruni's novel, *The Mistress of Spices,* portrays the protagonist, Tilo, as a financially independent woman who runs a spice store. She uses her knowledge of spices and clairvoyance to heal people and gain their trust. The novel explores the economic liberation of Tilo despite societal restrictions on women, and she redefines the traditional roles prescribed to women. In *Queen of Dreams*, the protagonist Rakhi, a successful businesswoman, inherits her mother's fortune as a means to escape her life of an unhappy marriage. The novel highlights women's agency to make business decisions and refuse to be financially dependent on their husbands. Divakaruni's novel *Oleander Girl* portrays the protagonist Korobi Roy and her experiences of economic independence when she starts working in a multinational company in the US. Her financial autonomy allows her to make decisions about her life and career that are not influenced by her family or societal restrictions. Economic independence facilitates women's ability to make independent decisions and satisfies their basic needs, as well as those of their families, without dependence on others. It also allows them to invest in their education and careers, providing them with better employment opportunities and security. This financial security provides them with the freedom to pursue entrepreneurship or take a break, if needed, without worrying about their financial stability.

In *The Mistress of Spices*, Tilo's economic independence grants her the freedom to fulfil her passion for helping people and to explore her self-realization. Her financial independence empowers her to make decisions about her life and career without external pressure or financial strain. Moreover, economic independence allows women to challenge the patriarchal attitudes and societal norms that are inclined to restrict their financial independence. Their financial autonomy empowers them to make decisions, control their own lives, and to negotiate for better wages and benefits. Divakaruni's novels portray women's struggle in achieving economic independence in the face of societal norms and patriarchal attitudes. Her works highlight women's financial autonomy as a means of achieving self-realization, making independent decisions, and challenging traditional gender roles. Economic independence provides women with both agency and security, enabling them to make informed decisions about their lives and careers. Divakaruni's representation of economically independent women also serves as an inspiration for others to strive for financial independence and self-empowerment.

Divakaruni's "Arranged Marriage" portrays the life of an Indian woman who is expected to conform to traditional gender roles and prioritize her family's needs over her own aspirations. The novel depicts how the cultural expectation of marriage and family life can limit women's ability to pursue education and employment, hindering their economic empowerment. In *Sister of My Heart*, the protagonist's mother expects her to conform to societal norms, including getting married and prioritizing her family's needs over her own. The novel highlights how cultural expectations for women can limit their access to education and, in turn, affect their employment opportunities and financial freedom. Divakaruni's *The Palace of Illusions* portrays Draupadi, the wife of the five Pandavas in the Indian epic, Mahabharata. The novel depicts how traditional gender roles limit Draupadi's economic freedom, as she is expected to fulfil the duties of a wife and mother. Her husband's desire to maintain social standing and suppresses Draupadi's ambitions, which hinders her from pursuing her career. The cultural expectations placed on women to prioritize their families over their careers serve as a significant barrier to their economic empowerment. Women face numerous hurdles, including a lack of access to education, limited job opportunities, and familial responsibilities such as childcare and household chores.

In *Sister of My Heart*, Anju's mother expects her to prioritize getting married instead of furthering her education. The cultural expectation of marriage and family life for women limits their access to education, which in turn affects their employment opportunities and ability to achieve economic empowerment. Moreover, the cultural expectations placed on women to prioritize their families' needs over their own often hinder their ability to pursue full-time employment or start their own businesses. Women's economic opportunities are limited when they are responsible for childcare and household chores, which often goes unrecognized and unpaid. Divakaruni's novels illustrate the impact of cultural expectations on women's ability to achieve economic empowerment. The societal norms and patriarchal attitudes that limit women's access to education, employment, and economic opportunities serve as significant hurdles. Her works highlight the need for cultural shifts that encourage women's economic ability and recognize their contributions to the economy. Divakaruni's novels show the urgent need to challenge these cultural expectations and support women's economic pursuits, whether it be through education, employment, or entrepreneurship.

Divakaruni's novel *The Mistress of Spices* portrays the life of Tilo, an Indian immigrant who runs a spice shop in Oakland, California. Tilo's family back home in India disapproves of her decision to immigrate to America and pursue her business, which they consider a lowly profession. The novel highlights the intergenerational divide that often exists in immigrant families and the difficulty that first-generation immigrants face in balancing their cultural traditions with pursuing their dreams. Tilo's family's disapproval of her occupation and life choices serves as a significant barrier to her economic empowerment. In *Sister of My Heart*, the protagonist Anju faces familial disapproval when she decides to pursue higher education. Anju's mother is hesitant to allow her daughter to study further, as she believes it will harm her chances of getting married. The novel shines a light on how societal norms and patriarchal expectations can limit women's access to education and, in turn, job opportunities. Divakaruni's *The Palace of Illusions* portrays Draupadi, the wife of the five Pandavas in the Indian epic, Mahabharata. The novel depicts how traditional gender roles limit Draupadi's economic freedom, as she is expected to fulfil the duties of a wife and mother. Her husband's desire to maintain social standing and suppresses Draupadi's ambitions, which hinders her from pursuing her career.

Familial expectations and societal norms that disapprove of women's involvement in economic pursuits serve as significant barriers to their financial empowerment. Women face numerous hurdles, including a lack of support, restricted access to capital, and limited education and employment opportunities. In *Mistress of Spices*, Tilo struggles to run her business due to her family's disapproval and her lack of access to capital. Bank loans require collateral, which Tilo's family has no interest in providing. Also, the societal norms of the conservative Indian community in which she lives in restrict her from directly interacting with her male customers. Therefore, her access to customers and revenue is limited. Moreover, disapproval from family or society can hamper women's ability to develop networks, form connections, gain knowledge, and pursue employment opportunities. This causes them to miss out on valuable, promising career opportunities that would provide them with economic empowerment. Divakurni's works explore the impact that disapproval from family and society can have on women, limiting their access to capital, education, and promising careers. They show the urgent need for a broader cultural shift where women's economic ability must be supported and encouraged by their families and society.

"Arranged Marriage" depicts the struggles of Indian immigrants in America, with particular attention to their economic hardships. The novel illuminates the complexities of the immigrant experience, highlighting the impact of economic inequality on their lives. Many of the characters face economic challenges that hamper their ability to achieve upward social mobility. Uma, the protagonist in "Arranged Marriage," struggles to make ends meet while living with her husband in Washington. The novel vividly demonstrates how economic inequality intensifies the difficulties of already marginalized groups. In *Queen of Dreams*, economic inequality is portrayed through the eyes of Rakhi, the novel's central character. Rakhi's economic situation deteriorates after her father's death, leaving her unable to maintain her family's financial stability. Similarly, Malini, the protagonist of *Sister of My Heart*, struggles with poverty as a result of her family's lack of economic power. Throughout the novel, Divakaruni emphasizes the limitations faced by people due to economic inequality, particularly women. Her novels showcase the barriers faced by individuals seeking to overcome economic inequality. Structural inequalities, oppressive social norms, and government policies all play a role in creating these barriers. Divakaruni poignantly portrays the challenges faced by individuals who must navigate these barriers daily.

For immigrants, language and cultural barriers are a significant challenge to their economic upliftment. Many characters in "Arranged Marriage" struggle to maintain employment while becoming acclimated to American customs. Similarly, in "Queen of Dreams," Rakhi's manoeuvring through complex social structures in America brings to light the difficulties faced by immigrants who seek to find their place in America's society and economy. Moreover, in *Sister of My Heart*, the characters deal with a lack of education and resources, which is often a significant barrier to upward mobility. The novel brings to light societal norms that keep women in a subservient role, limiting their access to education and job opportunities. The lack of education and resources also limits their ability to earn a higher income, perpetuating a cycle of economic inequality. Divakaruni's novels bring attention to the urgent issue of economic inequality. Her works showcase the difficulties of individuals attempting to navigate structural inequalities that impede their upward mobility. They provide a glimpse into the lives of those affected by economic inequality, highlighting the need for policy changes while calling for structural changes in society. They serve as a powerful reminder that economic inequality is more than just numbers; it is a pervasive issue that affects people's lives and well-being profoundly.

Divakaruni's novels bring to light the importance of women's representation in political contexts. Her works explore the deeply ingrained patriarchal structures that limit women's access to positions of power and the ways in which their absence from political structures perpetuates gender inequality. Women's representation in politics is essential for achieving gender equity in society. Women's voices need to be heard in decision-making, policy-making, and governance to ensure that their unique concerns and issues are addressed. However, gender-based discrimination severely limits women's access to political power and representation. In Divakaruni's *The Palace of Illusions*, women's representation in the political sphere is limited due to patriarchal constraints. Draupadi, the novel's central character, faces barriers at every turn as she attempts to exercise her political agency. The lack of representation of women in the political arena is a significant factor that hinders their ability to change policies and laws that restrict their rights and freedoms. Additionally, women's representation in political contexts is crucial for changing social norms and structures that perpetuate gender inequality. Through political power, women can challenge patriarchal systems and advocate for social and legal reforms that promote gender equity. In her novel *Sister of My Heart*, Divakaruni highlights the importance of women in politics through the character of Sudha, who desires to pursue a political career. Sudha's ambition is discouraged and even dismissed by her family members who believe that politics is a man's domain. The novel showcases how women's representation in politics is crucial for changing attitudes towards women's participation in spheres such as politics.

Women's representation in politics is not only crucial but also challenging. Patriarchal structures make it difficult for women to break into the male-dominated arena of politics. *The Palace of Illusions* highlights this challenge through Draupadi's struggle to achieve political representation. Patriarchy is so entrenched in society that men dismiss women's voices as unworthy, rendering their representation in politics a significant challenge. Furthermore, women in politics encounter numerous obstacles such as gender-based violence, discrimination, and sexist attitudes. Chitra Banerjee Divakaruni's novels expose these obstacles in creating an understanding of the complexity around women's political representation. They demonstrate that solving the issue of gender inequality requires addressing deeply ingrained patriarchal attitudes and norms that perpetuate discrimination against women in politics. They emphasize the importance of women's representation in political contexts. They highlight the dire need for women to play an active role in decision-making processes, governance, and policymaking. Through increasing women's representation in politics, social systems that perpetuate bias, prejudice, and discrimination can be reformed, leading to a more equitable society. Divakaruni's novels serve as a potent reminder that women's voices need to be heard in political contexts, and women must be provided with equal opportunities to participate in all aspects of political life.

Patriarchy is a social system that privileges men in positions of power, limiting the opportunities available to women. In political contexts, patriarchy often manifests in the form of gender-based discrimination, which undermines women's political agency and marginalizes their voices. Divakaruni's novels illuminate the ways in which women are affected by patriarchy in political contexts, highlighting the challenges they face in gaining access to positions of power. In *The Palace of Illusions*, Divakaruni retells the epic Mahabharata from the perspective of Draupadi, a female protagonist. Through Draupadi's story, the novel highlights the various ways in which patriarchy shapes women's experiences in politics. Notably, Draupadi's gender serves as a significant barrier to her political power, as she is expected to play a subordinate role within the male-dominated court. Despite her intelligence and determination, she is unable to gain access to positions of authority due to the deeply entrenched patriarchal norms that govern her society. Similarly, in *Sister of My Heart*, the character of Sudha dreams of pursuing a career in politics, but her interests are discouraged by her mother, who prioritizes traditional gender roles over political ambition. The novel exposes the ways in which patriarchy structures the social norms and expectations that constrain women's political potential.

Indeed, divisions of power promote and reinforce gender hierarchies, limiting women's political agency and making it difficult for them to attain or exercise political power. In this respect, patriarchy hinders women from accessing key political positions, undermining their political representation and visibility. In *The Palace of Illusions*, Draupadi's political agency is continuously threatened by patriarchy, as she faces various challenges that stand in the way of her ambitions. Daily routines, such as attending to men, cooking, or embroidery, as well as the socio-cultural expectations attached, become barriers to her participation in politics. Even when Draupadi attempts to assert her opinion or make decisions that would benefit her, she often finds that these efforts are undermined by the gendered expectations and attitudes of the men around her. Divakaruni's novels are a significant contribution to the discourse on gender and politics in patriarchal societies. Through her characters' experiences, she illuminates the ways in which gender-based discrimination and inequality intersect with politics to limit women's representation and political agency. Her works highlight the urgent need for greater gender parity in political contexts and call attention to the intersecting forms of discrimination that undermine women's political power. Ultimately, Divakaruni's novels serve as a powerful reminder of the importance of challenging patriarchal systems and promoting greater gender equity in all aspects of society.

Divakaruni explores how women's lives intersect with politics, revealing the constraints and limitations that they face. In *The Palace of Illusions*, Divakaruni retells the epic Mahabharata from the perspective of Draupadi, a female protagonist. Draupadi is portrayed as a strong and opinionated woman who is not afraid to voice her concerns and participate in political discussions. However, despite her unwavering determination and drive, her power is confined by the social norms of her time, which prohibit women from holding positions of political authority. Similarly, in *Sister of My Heart*, Divakaruni presents a vivid portrayal of Sudha, a young woman who dreams of pursuing a political career. However, her ambitions are stifled by societal expectations and her mother's traditional beliefs concerning gender and politics.

In *The Palace of Illusions*, the character of Panchaali is a prominent example of the limits of women's political power in her society. She is strong-willed, intelligent, and influential in her husband's court, yet her power is still bound by the norms and expectations of her society. In highlighting Panchaali's struggle for political agency, Divakaruni exposes the gender-based power dynamics that operate within Indian politics. In *Sister of My Heart*, Divakaruni portrays Sudha's desire to pursue a career in politics as something radical and subversive. Despite her intelligence and passion, Sudha's mother discourages her from pursuing her dreams, further underscoring the societal prejudices and gendered limitations that women face in politics. Divakaruni's novels offer valuable insights into the intersection of politics and gender in India. Her works reveal the enormous challenges that women encounter when trying to gain access to positions of political power, highlighting the need for greater gender parity in India's political sphere. By portraying characters like Draupadi, Panchaali, and Sudha, Divakaruni's novels demonstrate the intricate interplay between social norms, societal expectations, and the distribution of power within the political landscape. Ultimately, Divakaruni's work highlights the need for continued progress in addressing gender disparities in politics and serves as a powerful testament to the strength and resilience of women who fight for political equality.

India is a democratic country, but women's representation in politics is low. According to an article in The Hindu, only 22% of the Lok Sabha (lower house of the Parliament of India) consists of women. This gender imbalance is further perpetuated by patriarchal structures, cultural norms and social expectations that discourage women from participating in politics. Divakaruni's novels often deal with women's struggles to gain political agency and participate in decision-making processes. Her novel, *The Palace of Illusions,* retells the epic poem Mahabharata from the perspective of its female protagonist, Draupadi. In this novel, Divakaruni portrays Draupadi as a strong and opinionated woman who participates in political discussions and is vocal about her opinions, even in contexts where it is not widely accepted. However, despite her strength, Draupadi is still confined by the norms of her society, and her political power is limited. Similarly, in *Sister of My Heart*, Divakaruni portrays Sudha, who dreams of becoming a politician but is discouraged by her mother and social expectations. The limitations faced by Sudha highlight the challenges women face in entering fields dominated by men and the perpetuation of gender roles that limit women's potential.

In *The Palace of Illusions*, Divakaruni portrays the character of Panchaali, who is an example of the limitations faced by women in politics. Panchaali is a strong and outspoken woman, and her political significance is apparent in the court of her husbands, where she is an influential figurehead. However, her power is still confined by the norms of her society, which prevent her from taking full advantage of her influence. Panchaali's situation highlights the interplay between social norms and power dynamics, with these norms serving to restrict women's political power and maintain male dominance in the political sphere. Divakaruni's novels highlight the limitations faced by women in political contexts in India and shed light on the unequal power dynamics that restrict their political agency. While India has made significant progress in recent years towards gender parity in politics, there is still much work to be done to ensure that women have equal access to political representation and decision-making. Divakaruni's portrayal of strong female characters who challenge gender roles and social norms is a source of inspiration for women and a reminder of the ongoing struggle for gender parity in India.

India is a democratic country that has undergone significant political changes in recent years. However, women's political representation in the country remains low, with only 22% of the Lok Sabha being female representatives, according to an analysis in 2020. Women's access to political positions is further challenged by patriarchal structures, social norms and cultural expectations. Divakaruni's novels often depict women's struggles to gain political agency and participate in decision-making processes. Her novel *The Palace of Illusions* retells the epic poem Mahabharata through the eyes of its female protagonist, Draupadi. Divakaruni portrays Draupadi as a strong-willed woman who defies cultural norms by participating in political discussions and is vocal about her opinions, which is something not widely accepted in her society. Similarly, in *Sister of My Heart*, she portrays Sudha, who aspires to be a politician, but this dream is dashed by the social norms that prevent women from venturing into such fields. Sudha's mother tells her that "Politics is not for women. Women are too emotional to handle such a male-dominated field." These societal barriers force Sudha to turn away from politics and pursue a career in medicine instead.

The novel *The Palace of Illusions* is an excellent example of unequal power dynamics in political contexts in India. It is through the character of Panchaali that this political inequality is most apparent. Panchaali is a brave woman who is outspoken, yet her social and cultural norms confine her to the role of a wife. Panchaali's political significance is apparent in the court of her husbands, where she is an influential figurehead. However, she is restricted by the conventions of her society, which prevent her from taking full advantage of her influence. Panchaali's situation highlights the interplay between social norms and power dynamics, with these norms preventing women from fully exercising their political power. Divakaruni's works highlight the barriers faced by women in politics and the unequal power dynamics that restrict their political agency in India. Although India's political scene has undergone significant changes in recent years, women's access to political representation and decision-making remains limited. Divakaruni's portrayal of strong female characters who challenge these restrictions and gendered norms is an inspiration to women and contributes to the ongoing feminist struggle for gender parity in India.

Divakaruni's works highlight the unequal power dynamics and limitations faced by women in political contexts. Her novel, *The Mistress of Spices*, follows Tilo, a young Indian woman who uses the power of spices to control other people's lives. The novel subtly portrays Tilo's political skills as she manages the diverse customers that visit her spice shop, including politically influential people. Similarly, *One Amazing Thing* focuses on a group of strangers trapped in a visa office in the face of an earthquake. Among this group is Uma, an unemployed software engineer, who realizes her political consciousness as she narrates her experiences during the earthquake to help people come to terms with their immediate and ongoing realities. Divakaruni highlights the intersection between gender and politics, illustrating the effects of a patriarchal society that often denies women political agency. Her works underscore the importance of political representation for women, and the power dynamics that are a significant challenge for women's political involvement.

In her works, Divakaruni portrays women's experiences in economic contexts, highlighting the effects of social and economic inequality. *The Vine of Desire* portrays Sabitri Roy's story, who defies all odds to become a successful entrepreneur in Silicon Valley, despite familial disapproval and cultural expectations. Her novel, "Arranged Marriage," portrays the experiences of Indian women in America, particularly the challenges of adjusting to a new society and experiencing economic independence for the first time. Through these works, Divakaruni highlights the economic struggles faced by women, particularly in patriarchal societies that limit their access to resources and opportunities. By depicting women striving to overcome such circumstances, she emphasizes their resilience and ability to succeed despite the odds stacked against them. Divakaruni's portrayal of women in political and economic contexts is significant because it underscores the importance of advocating for women's rights and empowerment both in political and economic domains. By highlighting the challenges faced by women, particularly in developing countries or marginalized communities, she emphasizes the need for a gender-balanced political participation and decision-making process. Additionally, her portrayal of successful women in economic contexts serves as an inspiration and reinforces the need for equal access to resources and opportunities. Through her works, Divakaruni challenges gender stereotypes that have traditionally prevailed in politics and economics, promoting equality and advocating for the empowerment of women. She highlights the complex socio-political and economic systems that women navigate every day, and the challenges faced by women in these realms. Through her portrayal of strong-willed women who overcome these struggles, Divakaruni inspires and empowers women, underscoring the need for equal representation, empowerment, and advocating for equal access to opportunities and resources for both genders.

CHAPTER FOUR

PORTRAYAL OF WOMEN IN TERMS OF CULTURAL EXISTENCE

Chitra Banerjee Divakaruni is a prolific Indo-American writer who has explored the representation of women, particularly the challenges and opportunities they face in cultural contexts. Her novels have challenged stereotypical assumptions about women's roles and responsibilities, offering a nuanced portrayal of their lives. They are known for their depiction of female characters struggling to balance their personal aspirations with familial and societal expectations of them. Her novels delve into the complexities of women living in different cultural contexts and the challenges that they face as they strive to achieve their goals. In *The Palace of Illusions*, Draupadi, is shown grappling with the constraints of societal expectations. Draupadi is born into an aristocratic family, but her life takes a turn when she is forced to marry five brothers. The challenges she faces as a woman in a patriarchy society are highlighted in her struggle to claim autonomy and make decisions about her life. *Sister of My Heart* centers on the relationship between two cousins, Anju and Sudha, raised together in a conservative Indian family. Anju, the more progressive of the two, is determined to further her education and pursue a career, while Sudha is expected to marry and care for her family. The novel explores the conflict between individual aspirations and familial expectations in the context of a conservative society.

The portrayal of women in cultural contexts in Divakaruni's novels is significant because it highlights the diverse experiences of women. The novels explore how social, economic, and cultural factors impact women's daily lives, as well as their access to resources and opportunities. Women in traditional societies often face constraints that limit their agency and autonomy, and Divakaruni's novels bring visibility to these experiences. By portraying the challenges and limitations of the women living in cultures that prioritize patriarchal norms, she challenges the existing stereotypes of women and encourages readers to question patriarchal social norms. Divakaruni also celebrates the diversity of women's experiences and highlights the importance of the choices and decisions women make in their lives. In her novels, she emphasizes that women's lives are not one-dimensional, but are shaped by a myriad of factors such as social, economic, cultural, and historical contexts. She presents a nuanced view of women's experiences and the specific cultural contexts that shape them. By portraying the difficulties women face as they strive for autonomy and challenging traditional gender norms, Divakaruni encourages women to exercise their agency, make their own choices, and strive for their aspirations. Her works offer a vital contribution to highlighting the importance and diversity of women's experiences across cultures.

The novel *Queen of Dreams* portrays the economic oppression faced by Rakhi, the novel's protagonist. Rakhi, born and raised in a traditional Indian family in the USA, struggles to make ends meet while running her own business. Although she is a skilled artist and runs a successful business selling handmade sarees, she is not able to break free from the stereotypes and expectations imposed on women. Rakhi's business is dependent on a male-dominated industry, making it challenging to thrive. The men in the saree trade view her as an unwelcome competition and refuse to work with her. As a woman, Rakhi faces additional economic hurdles, including a lack of access to capital and loans. She is also forced to manage the double burden of work and household responsibilities despite being married and having a young child. Rakhi's experience illustrates how women's economic empowerment is characterized by significant challenges, particularly within traditional societies. Her story highlights the centrality of gender in shaping women's economic opportunities and the difficulties women face due to these cultural norms.

In *The Palace of Illusions*, Divakaruni also reflects on the economic oppression faced by women, as shown through Draupadi's story. The novel portrays a society that places little value on women's economic contribution. Women, even those born into wealth, have no economic agency and must depend on their fathers or husbands for financial support.

Draupadi, like Rakhi, must navigate through the oppressive forces of a male-dominated society. She is married to five brothers, but despite her status, she has no ownership over her wealth or land. Her economic power is significantly curtailed, rendering her financially vulnerable. Divakaruni emphasizes that women must use their voices to challenge the existing system and demand economic and social parity. By shedding light on the economic and social oppression faced by women in cultural contexts, Divakaruni unveils the oppressive forces that hinder their economic agency. She inspires women to claim their economic independence and to challenge the patriarchal culture that inhibits their growth.

One of her central themes is the oppression faced by women in these cultures, and she portrays the struggles and challenges women face while living within such systems. Through her distinctive writing style, Divakaruni highlights the cultural contexts and illustrates the harsh realities of women's oppression. *The Palace of Illusions* portrays the challenges faced by Draupadi due to the oppressive customs and practices in Hindu society. Draupadi belongs to a patriarchal society, where women are dependent on men for their identity and existence. Throughout the novel, she experiences oppression in various forms, from being forced into an arranged marriage to facing the brunt of male-dominated politics. Although Draupadi is a strong woman, capable of making her own decisions, she is repressed by the societal norms and traditions that govern her existence. She is forced to marry five brothers, and despite being a prized possession, she is continuously subjected to insults, mistreatment, and harassment. Despite all this, she refuses to be silenced and continues to speak up against the injustices done to her.

Sister of My Heart tells the story of two cousins, Anju and Sudha, who grow up together in a patriarchal society. The novel highlights the intense pressure and expectations placed on women to conform to societal norms. Both Anju and Sudha experience oppression in different forms. While Anju battles her husband's affair and society's expectations of marriage, Sudha resists conforming to cultural expectations and fights for her education. In their own ways, both women struggle to break free from the restrictive cultural norms that oppress them. Divakaruni's novels skilfully portray the intricacies of women's oppression in cultural contexts. Her characters' struggles and resilience provide insights into the impact of gender-based oppression on women living within patriarchal societies. Divakaruni's novels emphasize the importance of resistance against these oppressive systems and the need for women to assert their agency and independence. By portraying the challenges that women face and the ways in which they resist oppression, Divakaruni encourages women to stand up against societal norms that restrict their freedom and agency.

In *The Mistress of Spices*, Divakaruni portrays the story of a woman, Tilo, who resists the patriarchal norms that restrict her freedom. Through her knowledge of spices, Tilo empowers herself and other women who come to her spice shop. She also resists the romantic advances of the American man who falls in love with her, as she refuses to give up her freedom and independence. Similarly, in *The Palace of Illusions*, Divakaruni uses the character of Draupadi to portray women's resistance to patriarchy. Draupadi refuses to be the submissive wife society expects her to be and instead asserts her power and independence. She rebels against societal norms and refuses to remain silent when she is wronged, despite the consequences. In doing so, she becomes a symbol of feminine strength and resilience. Through her novels, Divakaruni portrays the complex and nuanced ways in which women resist oppressive structures. She shows that resistance can take many forms - it can be personal, individual, and quiet, or it can be collective, loud, and visible. Women's resistance can come in the form of education, career, personal relationships, and refusing to comply with societal norms and expectations. By portraying women who resist oppression and assert their power and independence, Divakaruni's novels inspire and empower women to challenge oppressive structures and reclaim their agency within patriarchal societies.

The Palace of Illusions explores the ways in which Draupadi and other female characters face different forms of oppression within patriarchal societies. Draupadi is forced into a marriage she does not want, and she experiences multiple disempowering incidents throughout her life, including being publicly humiliated and physically assaulted. Her experiences highlight how women in traditional societies are restricted by patriarchal structures and are often treated as inferior beings. Furthermore, the novel depicts how social norms, including marriage, dowry, and women's purity, are used to control and oppress women. Princess Amba's character is an example of how societal norms and traditions can also make women vulnerable to oppression. Amba is not allowed to marry the man of her choice, and the system fails to give her any agency, which ultimately leads to her destruction. It underscores the importance of acknowledging the oppression of women and their agency in reshaping patriarchal norms.

Divakaruni's work highlights the need to empower women to find their voice and challenge oppressive social structures that constrain their progress. Through the story of Draupadi and the other female characters, Divakaruni's work shows the value of women and their contributions to society and emphasizes the need for cultural change to support and uplift women.

In *The Mistress of Spices*, Divakaruni explores the tension between traditional Indian values and modern Western culture. The novel tells the story of Tilo, a young Indian woman who possesses the power to heal and transform people's lives through the mystical powers of spices she sells in her spice shop. The story explores how Tilo struggles to reconcile her traditional roots and her attraction to modern Western culture. She is drawn to modernity, which is counter to traditional Indian values that discourage such behavior. She is caught between fulfilling her obligations as an Indian woman and her desire to live her life on her own terms. The novel presents the clash between tradition and modernity, where Tilo finds herself in a complex struggle to balance the old world and the new. In *Sister of My Heart*, Divakaruni portrays the clash between traditional Indian practices and modern Western influence. The novel follows the lives of two cousins, Anju and Sudha, who are raised in Calcutta by their families. The novel focuses on the conflict between Indian traditions and modern values, which are prevalent in the lives of both Anju and Sudha. Anju's family is more traditional and believes in arranged marriages, while Sudha's family is more progressive and has different views on arranged marriages. The novel shows how the girls' lives are affected by their families' differing attitudes towards what is traditional and what is modern, ultimately depicting the differences between living in traditional and modern India.

Queen of Dreams is a novel that explores the clash between modern and traditional values from a mother and daughter's perspective. The story follows Rakhi and her mother, who are both grappling with issues surrounding identity and the tension between traditional and modern values. Rakhi's mother, who is haunted by dreams of her past, is seen as the keeper of her family's traditional values, while Rakhi straddles the line between embracing modernity and upholding traditional Indian values. The novel shows how this tension between tradition and modernity plays out in the lives of the characters, ultimately depicting how these struggles shape the Indian American experience. Divakaruni's work highlights the importance of adapting to changing times while still respecting one's cultural heritage, navigating the delicate balance between traditions and modern values.

In *The Palace of Illusions*, through Draupadi's perspective, Divakaruni exposes the discrimination and oppression of women in a period of history characterized by male dominance. Draupadi was constantly objectified, and her voice was silenced by the men in her life. Despite her intelligence and capabilities, the authority figures in Draupadi's life never allowed her to reveal her full potential, in part due to patriarchal norms. *Sister of My Heart* is a novel that follows the lives of two cousins, Anju and Sudha, who grew up together in Calcutta. The story depicts the patriarchal oppression of women in traditional Indian families where women's roles were restricted by the norms and expectations of their husband's family. Divakaruni provides insights into the lives of women in traditional Indian families where a wife's obedience to her husband is considered paramount. Anju's father, who came from a conservative family, married a strong, independent woman, much to the disapproval of his family. As a result, his children were subjected to their family's ire and tyranny to keep them in line with traditional gender roles. The family's patriarchal attitudes restricted access to education and job opportunities, forcing the girls to marry young in arranged marriages.

One Amazing Thing features a diverse cast of characters, each with a different background and story. The novel portrays the patriarchal oppression of women, even in modern and westernized contexts. Through the experiences of Uma and her mother, Divakaruni highlights the issues that arise when societal norms and expectations compete with modern feminist ideals. For example, Uma's mother had always wanted to be an artist but wasn't allowed to pursue her ambitions because of her gender. She, therefore, had to give up her dreams to conform to her community's patriarchal norms. Divakaruni's works emphasize the theme of patriarchal oppression of women in different cultural contexts where society's norms and traditions perpetuate gender inequality. Her novels provide insights into the struggles of women navigating patriarchal systems and the impact of such hardship on their lives. By focusing on this theme, Divakaruni sheds light on the cultural complexities of life in South Asia and beyond. Her work highlights the importance of societal reform and more equitable social structures that empower women to realize their potential.

Sister of My Heart portrays the struggles of Anju and Sudha as they navigate their lives within an oppressive patriarchal system. The societal restrictions on women's education, career opportunities, and the constant pressure to marry are all highlighted through the life stories of the two cousins. *The Palace of Illusions* explores the social issues of gender bias, women empowerment, and patriarchy in ancient Indian society. Divakaruni provides insights into the struggles of women in a period of history characterized by male dominance.The novel portrays the harsh realities of a woman's life in ancient India, where Draupadi is forced to accept the status quo dictated by men. Through Draupadi's perspective, Divakaruni exposes the systemic abuse and oppression of women who had limited control over their own lives, bodies, and futures. *Oleander Girl* explores the social issues of class differences, cultural assimilation, and generational conflicts. Divakaruni provides insights into the struggles of individuals belonging to different social classes and cultures in contemporary Indian society.The novel portrays the struggles of Korobi, who must confront her family's hidden past and learn to navigate unfamiliar situations, including adapting to different cultures and social circles. Divakaruni highlights the tensions that exist between different social classes, the problems they face due to societal expectations and traditions, and the impact of these problems on individual lives. The theme of social issues in cultural contexts is a reoccurring motif in Chitra Banerjee Divakaruni's novels, addressing problems such as gender bias, patriarchal systems, class differences, cultural assimilation, and the caste system. Her works emphasize the importance of societal understanding and acceptance, highlighting the need for breaking the shackles of societal standards and conventions which limit the opportunities of social groups. By shedding light on these themes, Divakaruni provides a unique perspective on cultural and social issues, illustrating the challenges and hopes of individuals belonging to different social groups.

In *The Mistress of Spices*, Divakaruni portrays the cultural disparity that Tilo experiences as she feels caught between two worlds. Tilo's experiences are representative of the challenges faced by immigrants as they try to navigate their way in a new culture. She must learn to adjust to the new culture while still maintaining her traditional values. Queen of Dreams explores the relationship between a mother, Rakhi, and her daughter, Jazmin. Rakhi, an Indian immigrant, is haunted by her past and is unable to assimilate into American culture, while Jazmin, who was raised in America, is unable to relate to her mother's traditions. Divakaruni portrays the cultural disparity between the mother and daughter as they have grown up in different cultural contexts. Their struggle to understand each other's perspectives exemplifies how cultural differences can become a barrier to communication and understanding.

One Amazing Thing is set in an American consulate in an unidentified South Asian country. The novel follows the stories of nine strangers who become trapped together after an earthquake. The characters come from varied backgrounds, and their differences are highlighted by the cultural disparity among them. Divakaruni portrays the cultural disparity among the characters as they struggle to communicate and understand each other's perspectives. The novel highlights how, even in a cosmopolitan setting, cultural differences can be a source of tension and conflict. The theme of cultural disparity among women in cultural contexts is prevalent in Divakaruni's novels. Her works highlight how traditional societies can clash with progressive values, leading to cultural alienation and displacement for women. By portraying these themes, Divakaruni provides insights into the struggles of immigrants as they try to navigate and balance their cultural values and assimilation into a new culture. Her works emphasize the importance of understanding and accepting cultural differences for the sustainable coexistence of people from different backgrounds in society.

In *The Palace of Illusions* is a retelling of the Mahabharata from the perspective of Draupadi. As a princess, Draupadi has been brought up in luxury and comfort, but when she is forced to marry the five Pandava brothers, she becomes a Low Power Bride. She has little say in her own life and is defined by her husbands' choices, decisions, and actions. Divakaruni portrays Low Power Brides as women who are subject to the patriarchal system imposed upon them by society. Draupadi's character is a window into the challenges faced by women in arranged marriages, where the men hold all the power and women have to navigate a new and different power dynamic. *Sister of My Heart* revolves around two cousins, Anju and Sudha, who are raised together but marry different men. Anju becomes a Low Power Bride when her in-laws force her to leave her career to pursue her duties as a wife and mother. Divakaruni portrays Low Power Brides as women who are caught up in the conflicts between their own identities and their families' expectations. Anju is adept at balancing her roles as a wife, mother, and daughter-in-law, but this comes at the cost of her own happiness and sense of self.

Divakaruni's collection of short stories, "Arranged Marriage," delves into the lives of women who are thrown into arranged marriages with men they hardly know. The stories explore the psychological, physical, and emotional toll of arranged marriages and how women navigate these marriages. Divakaruni portrays Low Power Brides as women who are forced to make compromises to maintain peace in their marriages. In "The Silver Pavements," the protagonist Sita is shocked when she discovers that her husband married her to obtain an American green card. Sita feels trapped, but she manages to navigate a way out of the marriage with the support of her sister. Divakaruni's novels highlight the struggles of women in cultural contexts as Low Power Brides in their marriages. Her works emphasize the challenges and compromises that women face when they are forced into arranged marriages, and how they navigate them. Through her characters' experiences, she sheds light on the power dynamic between men and women in traditional societies and how women find ways to assert their will within those confines. By portraying Low Power Brides in her novels, Divakaruni provides a voice to the plight of women in traditional societies and the struggles they face as they try to find their place in the world.

In *The Mistress of Spices*, the protagonist Tilo is deeply connected to her Indian heritage through her love for spices. As a mistress of spices, Tilo has a unique ability to connect with people and help them with their problems through the use of spices. Her love for Indian culture is evident in her appreciation for the healing properties of spices and the importance of their use in Indian cuisine. Divakaruni portrays the love for Indian culture as a way for women in cultural contexts to maintain a connection to their roots. Tilo's use of spices to heal and connect people reflects the importance of preserving cultural heritage and utilizing its resources to enhance one's life in a new society. In *Queen of Dreams*, the protagonist Rakhi is torn between her desire to fit in with her American friends and her love for Indian culture. She struggles to reconcile her mother's visions of the future, which are rooted in Hindu mythology, with her own sense of self as an American teenager. Divakaruni portrays the love for Indian culture as a way for women in cultural contexts to connect with their families and their past. Rakhi's mother's visions of the future connect her to her mother's heritage, and her own sense of self is shaped by her mother's values and beliefs.

In "Arranged Marriage," Divakaruni's collection of short stories, many of the female protagonists are immigrants or first-generation Americans struggling to balance their love for Indian culture with the realities of their lives in America. For example, in the story "Clothes," the protagonist has a deep attachment to the clothes of her homeland, but she knows that wearing them would draw unwanted attention in America. Divakaruni portrays the love for Indian culture as a way for women in cultural contexts to maintain a sense of identity in the face of assimilation pressures. The clothes and other customs from their homeland serve as reminders of their cultural roots and provide comfort and familiarity in a new society. Divakaruni's novels showcase the love for Indian culture among women in cultural contexts. Her works highlight the complexities of balancing cultural heritage with the realities of life in America. Through her characters' experiences, she emphasizes the importance of preserving cultural traditions while also adapting to a new society. By showing the love for Indian culture as a unifying force among women in cultural contexts, she gives voice to the struggles and joys of the immigrant experience.

Divakaruni's novels are known for exploring the complexities of immigrant experiences and the challenges of assimilating and acculturating to a new society. In "Arranged Marriage," the collection of short stories by Divakaruni, many of the female protagonists are immigrants or first-generation Americans trying to assimilate into the dominant culture. For example, in the story "The Silver Pavements," the protagonist has to adjust to the fast-paced lifestyle of America, compared to the slower pace of life in India. Divakaruni portrays the struggle of assimilation as a common experience among women in cultural contexts. The pressure to conform to the dominant culture can be overwhelming and lead to a loss of one's cultural identity. Through her characters' experiences, she gives voice to the complexities of navigating between two cultures. In *Queen of Dreams*, the protagonist Rakhi must reconcile her Indian heritage with her American identity. Rakhi struggles to understand her mother's visions of the future while juggling the reality of her everyday life in America. Divakaruni portrays the process of acculturation as not just a matter of adapting to a new culture but also a matter of reconciling one's identity with one's cultural heritage. Rakhi's journey of self-discovery highlights the complexities of negotiating between two cultures and the internal conflicts that arise as a result. In *The Mistress of Spices*, Divakaruni highlights the concept of hybridity as a way for women in cultural contexts to create new identities that blend elements of their cultural heritage and their experiences in a new society. Tilo's use of spices, which represent her cultural roots, is a way for her to retain a connection to her homeland while also adapting to her new environment. Divakaruni's novels explore the themes of assimilation and acculturation among women in cultural contexts. She portrays the challenges of navigating between two cultures as a common experience among women from immigrant backgrounds. By highlighting the complexities of this experience, she gives voice to the struggles and conflicts that arise as people try to reconcile their cultural heritage with their experiences in a new society. Through her characters‘ journeys, she emphasizes the importance of creating new, hybrid identities that blend cultural elements from both worlds.

Chitra Banerjee Divakurni's novels are known for their exploration of the lives of women in cultural contexts. One recurring theme in her works is the sense of nostalgia and love for homeland that characters experience, particularly among women. In *The Mistress of Spices*, Divakurni shows how Tilo's love for her homeland is manifested through the spices, which remind her of home and bring her a sense of comfort and familiarity. Through Tilo's character, we see how women in modern societies yearn for the comfort of their cultural roots, especially when they are far from home. In *The Palace of Illusions*, Draupadi expresses her love for her homeland through her unwavering devotion to her husband, Arjuna. She remains committed to him, despite the challenges they face while living in exile, because her love for him is tied to her deep love for her homeland, India. Divakurni portrays Draupadi's love for India as a symbol of her identity and values as a woman from a cultural context. Her patriotism illustrates how women can have deep connections to their homeland, linking their sense of self to their culture and values. In *Sister of My Heart*, Anju, the protagonist, yearns for her homeland in India and longs for a return to her childhood memories. She is faced with the contrast of her past life of abundance and the present life, which is marked by economic struggles and adjustment to a new country. Divakurni highlights Anju's sense of nostalgia as a universal theme experienced by people of different ages and cultural backgrounds. She represents the nostalgia that people experience when they feel disconnected from their roots and long for familiarity, comfort, and continuity. She shows how women relate to cultural symbols and use them to connect with their home countries and cultural roots. From Tilo's spices in *The Mistress of Spices* to Draupadi's patriotism in *The Palace of Illusions*, Divakurni explores the often-complex relationships between women and their countries of origin. Through her works, she highlights the importance of cultural identity, the desire for continuity, and the impact of cultural dislocation on individuals' sense of self.

In *The Mistress of Spices*, Divakurni explores the central character Tilo's isolation and loneliness, as she must live a solitary life in order to perform her duties as a mistress of spices. Despite her remarkable abilities and powers, Tilo lives a life of intense loneliness and yearns for connection with others. Divakurni portrays Tilo's loneliness as a result of societal structures that require her to live a life of isolation, where she can only connect with others through the herbs and spices she administers. Tilo's loneliness highlights the idea that women's roles and duties in some cultures demand that they live lives of isolation and seclusion in order to fulfil their traditional roles. In *The Palace of Illusions*, Divakurni portrays the protagonist Draupadi's sense of loneliness and isolation, as she is married to the five Pandava brothers but does not have any other female companionship in her life. Her husbands maintain a singular focus on their own relationships with her, leaving her to feel lonely and unfulfilled in her role as a wife. Divakurni portrays the plight of women in patriarchal cultures as one of profound loneliness, especially when women are expected to conform to traditional gender roles, which limit their social circles and personal fulfilment.

In *Sister of My Heart*, Divakurni explores the isolation and loneliness of the central character, Anju. Despite growing up with her cousin Sudha, who is like a sister to her, Anju still experiences a sense of isolation and loneliness due to societal pressures, which require her to marry and start a family. Divakurni portrays the loneliness experienced by Anju as a result of societal expectations of women and their inability to break free from societal norms. Women like Anju are trapped in a society where their worth is determined by their ability to conform to societal standards, which can lead to intense loneliness and isolation. Divakurni highlights the experiences of women who live in patriarchal cultures, where societal expectations and gender roles can limit their social connections and personal fulfilment. Divakurni portrays the isolation and loneliness experienced by these women as a result of cultural norms and societal expectations that set them apart from the rest of society. Through her portrayal of loneliness, Divakurni encourages readers to reflect on the importance of social connections and the need for cultural change to create a more inclusive and fulfilling society for all.

In *The Palace of Illusions*, Divakurni portrays the myth of the Mahabharata as a cautionary tale of the dangers of pride and ambition. The central character, Draupadi, is portrayed as a woman with great pride and ambition, which leads to her downfall. Despite her role as the queen, she is not immune to the limitations and discriminations faced by women in a patriarchal society. Divakurni uses the myth of Mahabharata to highlight the role and limitations of women in the story and their struggles in a male-dominated society. In *The Mistress of Spices*, Divakurni uses elements of Indian mythology to create a magical and fantastical world that is enchanting to readers. The protagonist, Tilo, is a mistress of spices and has the power to change people's lives through the herbs that she administers to them. The story is a reimagining of the Hindu goddess of the spices, Annapurna, who is believed to embody the power of food. Divakurni uses mythology to create a magical realism experience for the readers, blurring the lines between the real and supernatural worlds. Through Tilo's character, the author explores the relationship between people and nature, and how nature can have a profound impact on our lives. Furthermore, mythology is used to comment on the value of individuality, as Tilo's power lies within being different from others.

In *The Vine of Desire*, Divakurni uses the Hindu mythology of the goddess Kali to comment on the complexities of love, motherhood, and womanhood. The protagonist, Anju, discovers her husband's infidelity and must navigate the complexities of marriage, motherhood, and love in a patriarchal society. Divakurni employs the myth of Kali to explore the darker side of human emotions and behavior, as well as to provide commentary on female empowerment and the value of femininity. Moreover, the myth of Kali allows Divakurni to explore the idea of rebirth and transformation in women's lives, suggesting that women have the power to rise above the challenges they face and come out stronger on the other side. Divakurni's novels re-imagine ancient myths and legends from the viewpoint of women, revealing the struggles, aspirations, and limitations faced by women in different cultures. Through her portrayal of myth, Divakurni highlights the complexities of culture and the impact that it has on the lives of people who are affected by it. Her works encourage women to challenge cultural norms and assert their rights, despite the challenges and hardships that they may face.

Divakurni's novels have been praised for their ability to portray the struggles of women in patriarchal societies, and the ways in which oppressive cultural norms dictate women's behavior. They explore the dislocation of women in cultural contexts, highlighting the challenges and complexities that women encounter. In *The Mistress of Spices*, Tilo encounters significant dislocation as she struggles to adjust to her new environment. Tilo's character is dislocated from her Indian identity as she attempts to navigate an unfamiliar culture, yet she is simultaneously compelled to maintain her cultural heritage. Through Tilo's character, Divakurni conveys the struggles that immigrant women face in adjusting to a new society while preserving their cultural identity. Furthermore, Tilo is dislocated from her role as a woman in her patriarchal culture. She was expected to marry a man who could provide for her financially and father her children. Instead of adhering to these expectations, Tilo pursued her passion for spices, disobeying the patriarchal norms that governed her society. Tilo struggles to reconcile her desires with the expectations placed upon her by society, highlighting the hardships that arise when women challenge cultural norms. The various dislocations that Tilo faces in the novel demonstrate the complexities involved in being a woman in a new culture.

In *The Palace of Illusions*, Divakurni tackled the concept of dislocation in a different manner. In the book, she portrays the life of Draupadi, the wife of five brothers, who seeks justice and empowerment in a society that oppresses women. Draupadi is dislocated from the patriarchal society of ancient India, which objectifies women and demands their subservience. Divakurni highlights the powerlessness that women face as they attempt to navigate cultural norms that are designed to reinforce male dominance. Through Draupadi's experience, Divakurni illustrates how women in patriarchal societies are systematically dislocated from positions of power and influence. Draupadi, as a woman, is stripped of her agency and reduced to an object to be bartered, reinforcing the limitations placed on women in patriarchal societies. Draupadi's story is a poignant reminder of how dislocation in cultural contexts can limit a woman's ability to control her own life.

In *The Vine of Desire*, Divakurni explored the dislocation of women within the context of marriage and motherhood. The protagonist, Anju, is dislocated from her desires and aspirations as she struggles to reconcile her ambitions with the cultural expectations of her community. Anju's community demands that she marries, has children, and becomes a homemaker, but she aspires for more than this. Anju's character highlights the limitations placed on women's choices within patriarchal societies, a dislocation that can lead to unfulfilled aspirations for women. Furthermore, Divakurni demonstrates the complexities of cultural dislocation for Indian immigrant women in America. Like in *The Mistress of Spices*, Divakurni's character is forced to reconcile her Indian heritage with American culture. Anju's position as an immigrant woman in America adds another layer of dislocation to her experiences, exposing the unique challenges that immigrant women face.

Divakurni's works serve as a window into the cultural existence of women and how society's expectations affect their behavior. She portrayed women who battle the influence of their culture and the patriarchal society. In *The Mistress of Spices*, Divakurni portrays an Indian woman, Tilo, who is struggling to navigate American culture while preserving her Indian identity. Tilo, an immigrant, works in an Oakland spice shop selling spices and herbs that possess magical properties, which she uses to help other women. Through Tilo's character, Divakurni highlights the challenges that immigrant women face in adjusting to a new culture while preserving their cultural identity. In *The Palace of Illusions*, Divakurni portrays Draupadi, a character in the Indian epic, the Mahabharata, who is married to five brothers. Her character demonstrates how cultural norms can affect a woman's life, leading to exploitation and abuse. Divakurni uses Draupadi's character to show the subservience of women to the patriarchal society and how women are objectified in the Indian society.

The Vine of Desire depicts the cultural norms and societal expectations placed on Indian women regarding marriage and motherhood. Anju, the protagonist, struggles to reconcile her ambitions and desires with the cultural expectations of her community, which demand that she marries, bear children, and be a homemaker. The novel demonstrates how cultural norms influence women's decision-making, limiting their choices and restricting their freedom. In her works, Divakurni portrays the cultural existence of women and the ways in which patriarchal societies function to oppress women. Her stories depict the difficulties that women face in preserving their cultural identity while challenging cultural norms that limit their growth and development. Through her characters, Divakurni highlights the importance of women embracing their cultural identity and making themselves heard in a patriarchal society. Her stories depict the struggles of women against cultural norms that limit their aspirations and opportunities. Divakurni emphasizes the importance of women asserting themselves and breaking free from oppressive patriarchal structures, while also highlighting the significance of preserving cultural identity. Her works contribute to the empowerment of women and provide a perspective on the challenges faced by women in navigating their cultural existence in patriarchal societies.

CHAPTER FIVE

WOMEN OF DIVAKURNI'S WORLD IN CONTEXT OF SOCIAL MILIEU

Chitra Banerjee Divakurni's literary works offer a clear insight into the social milieu of the patriarchal society and the impact of such a society on the woman. Her novels offer a critical analysis of the struggles of women within the patriarchal structures that exist in traditional societies. Divakurni highlights the need for women to assert themselves, finding their voice, and take control of their lives to combat the prevalent patriarchal domination in the society. Divakurni's literary works depict women as victims of patriarchal domination under societal norms and expectations. In *The Palace of Illusions*, the author portrays female characters such as Draupadi facing societal oppression, neglect, and abuse at the hands of men. Draupadi is forced to marry five brothers and is later humiliated in public. Divakurni portrays Draupadi's traumatic experiences and highlights the patriarchal society's objectification of women as possessions rather than individuals with free will and agency. In her novel, *The Mistress of Spices*, Divakurni depicts the challenges faced by Indian immigrant women in the United States. The protagonist, Tilo, is an immigrant woman who works as a spice seller in Oakland. Through Tilo's character, the author highlights the struggles of immigrant women, including societal isolation, cultural conflict, and the patriarchal expectation of women's subservience to men. The novel highlights the importance of preserving one's culturaMENl identity while adapting to a new society. In *The Vine of Desire*, Divakurni highlights the struggles of Anju, who tries to navigate societal expectations to marry and have children. Anju faces significant challenges as she struggles to reconcile her individual desires and ambitions with the society's patriarchal norms. Divakurni portrays the need for women to resist the patriarchal structures that limit their aspirations and opportunities, asserting their identities and striving to achieve their goals.

Divakurni's literary works emphasize the significance of women finding their voice and asserting themselves to combat patriarchal domination. She portrays strong female characters who assert their identities and challenge societal norms to inspire women to take control of their lives and break free from oppressive patriarchal structures. By delineating women's struggles within the traditional patriarchal society, Divakurni inspires women to challenge societal norms or norms that prevent them from achieving their full potential. Her novels highlight the struggles of women within traditional societies and the need for women to assert themselves, find their voice, and take control of their lives. By portraying strong female characters that resist patriarchal structures, Divakurni inspires women to challenge societal norms that limit their aspirations and opportunities. Her literary work stresses the liberation of women from societal patriarchal domination, ultimately contributing to the empowerment of women. Throughout her works, Divakurni highlights the struggles of women within the restrictive and oppressive social structures that exist in traditional societies. Her female characters often face discrimination, neglect, and abuse at the hands of men. By depicting these struggles, Divakurni highlights the importance of understanding the systemic oppression of women in such societies, and the role of women themselves in pushing back against it. One of her most notable works, *The Palace of Illusions*, is a retelling of the Indian epic, *The Mahabharata*, from the point of view of its main female character, Draupadi. The story highlights the struggles of Draupadi, who is forced to marry five brothers and is later humiliated in public. Through Draupadi's character, Divakurni shows how women in patriarchal societies are seen as property and disposable possessions, rather than individuals with free will and agency. In her novel, *The Mistress of Spices*, Divakurni depicts the challenges faced by Indian immigrant women in the United States. The protagonist, Tilo, is an immigrant woman who works as a spice seller in Oakland. Through Tilo's character, the author highlights the struggles of women who are caught between two worlds, the traditional world of their heritage and the modern world of America. The novel highlights the importance of preserving one's cultural identity while adapting to a new society. Divakurni's novels also highlight the importance of women finding their voices and asserting their identities. In *The Vine of Desire*, the protagonist, Anju, must navigate through societal pressures to marry and have children, while also struggling with her own desires and ambitions. By highlighting Anju's struggles, Divakurni emphasizes the importance of women speaking up for themselves and taking control of their lives, even in the face of societal expectations. Her works highlight the struggles of women in traditional societies and the importance of women's empowerment. By portraying strong female characters who assert their identities and challenge societal norms, Divakurni inspires women to take control of their lives, find their voices, and break free from oppressive patriarchal societies.

Her novels and short stories portray the experiences of women confronting cultural and social norms that reinforce male dominance and control, examining how patriarchal structures are embedded within broader systems of inequality and oppression. In *The Palace of Illusions*, Draupadi is born into a patriarchal society, where women are relegated to subservient roles and are often subject to men's control and abuse. As she grows up, she becomes a strong, independent woman, defying traditional gendered roles and asserting her agency in the face of patriarchal oppression. Divakaruni's retelling of the epic through the lens of a female protagonist critiques the representation of women in the original story and challenges the patriarchal norms and values inherent in classical Indian literature. Divakaruni's works often explore the deep bonds of women friendships, especially in the context of the social milieu. Her novels and short stories often portray complex relationships and connections between women that arise from shared experiences of navigating societal norms, obstacles, and opportunities. One of Divakaruni's most popular works that explores women friendships in context of the social milieu is *Sister of my Heart*. This novel tells a story of two girls, Anju and Sudha, who grow up in Calcutta, India, and form a close bond that is as deep as sisters. The novel traces the trajectories of their lives as they tackle the challenges of growing up in a highly patriarchal society, with encounters with arranged marriages, classism, and societal pressures. The novel portrays how the women's friendship provides a sanctuary in a world where they feel isolated and ignored, giving them the courage to resist stereotypes and seek out their identities. Another example of Divakaruni's portrayal of women's friendships in context of the social milieu can be seen in her short story "The Maid Servant's Story." It is a story of the friendship between two maids, one from a rural background and the other from the city, who come to work in a rich household in Calcutta. The story follows their experiences in this household, including the challenges of the rigid class system and the sociocultural norms that prevent them from achieving their dreams. The women's friendship provides solace and support in the face of these challenges.

In *Queen of Dreams*, Divakaruni portrays the relationship between a mother and a daughter that is bound by their capacity to shape dreams. Rakhi, the protagonist, has a tumultuous relationship with her mother, who once ran an unusual dream interpretation business. The novel explores how their relationship evolves over time as they confront their traumas, losses, and deepest fears. Rakhi's realization of her mother's enduring resilience and strength helps her come to terms with her own dreams, within the broader framework of the social and cultural milieu she inhabits. Through these and other examples, Divakaruni's works demonstrate a nuanced and empathetic depiction of women's friendships in context of the social milieu. Her writings capture the subtleties of women's social networks that emerge out of shared experiences of social hierarchies, gender norms, and economic realities. They illustrate how friendships serve as crucial sites for support, comfort, and resistance against the systemic oppressions and exclusive hierarchies of the larger society. Divakaruni's works offer a powerful examination and exploration of women's friendships in the context of the social milieu. Across her novels and short stories, she highlights the vital role that these deep bonds of friendship play in providing sanctuary, support, and resistance for women negotiating the often-deeply-entrenched societal norms, hierarchies, and expectations. Her works provide important insights into the subtleties of these relationships, and the complexity of women's lives in the broader social and cultural contexts in which they occur.

Her novels and short stories portray the often-complicated dynamics that exist between mothers and daughters, particularly those living within the context of the Indian diaspora. Through her works, Divakaruni highlights the cultural and societal expectations and pressures that impact these relationships. One example of the portrayal of mother-daughter relationships in Divakaruni's works can be seen in her novel, *The Vine of Desire*. The story follows Anju and Sudha, two women who come from different socio-economic backgrounds but are brought together by the bonds of their friendship. Anju and Sudha's mothers have vastly different expectations for their daughters, with Anju's mother placing a great emphasis on education and social status, while Sudha's mother values more traditional roles for her daughter. The novel explores how these expectations shape Anju and Sudha's sense of identity and their relationship with their mothers. The novel portrays the subtle and not-so-subtle conflicts that can arise from these differing expectations and the impact that it can have on the mother-daughter relationship. Another example of the portrayal of mother-daughter relationships in Divakaruni's works can be seen in the short story "Clothes." The story follows Sumita, a young bride who has moved from India to the United States. Sumita's mother has chosen her wedding dress, which is traditional and conservative, but Sumita wishes to wear a more modern and fashionable dress. The story highlights the tension that arises from the differing expectations and priorities of Sumita and her mother. It also portrays the impact that societal and cultural norms and expectations can have on mother-daughter relationships.

In "Arranged Marriage," Divakaruni's collection of short stories, the theme of mother-daughter relationships is also evident. In the story "The Silver Pavements," the protagonist is a young girl named Mona who moves to the United States with her family. Mona's mother has high expectations for her daughter and wants her to achieve success in her academic pursuits. However, Mona struggles to reconcile these expectations with her own desires and interests. The story highlights the complexity of mother-daughter relationships and the impact that cultural and societal expectations can have on these relationships. Through her works, Divakaruni portrays the mother-daughter relationship as a complex one that is shaped by many factors, including societal norms, cultural traditions, and individual expectations. She highlights the tensions that can arise from these differing expectations and the impact that it can have on the mother-daughter relationship. Divakaruni's works also underscore the need to challenge these norms and expectations and to work towards a more equitable and just society and relationships between mothers and daughters. Divakurni, through her works, highlights the challenges faced by individuals from lower socio-economic backgrounds as they navigate their way in a society that is often dominated by those from wealthier and more privileged backgrounds. She draws attention to the inequalities and social hierarchies that exist in the South Asian diaspora and the United States and the impact that these hierarchies have on people's lives. One example of class distinction in Divakaruni's work can be seen in her novel, *One*

Amazing Thing. The story follows a group of individuals who are trapped in a visa office in California during an earthquake. As they wait for help, they begin to share stories about their lives. The protagonist, Uma, is a graduate student from India who is working in the visa office. Uma comes from a middle-class family and has always been taught to work hard to achieve her goals. However, she quickly realizes that in the United States, her degree may not be enough to secure her a good job. She struggles to reconcile her expectations with the reality of life in America, where class distinctions are more pronounced. In "Arranged Marriage," Divakaruni's collection of short stories, the theme of class distinction is also evident. In the story "Mrs. Dutta Writes a Letter," the titular character is an elderly woman who has moved to the United States to live with her son and his family. Mrs. Dutta is from a wealthy background in India and has always enjoyed a position of privilege. However, in America, she finds herself struggling to adapt to a new and different way of life. She feels out of place in her son's middle-class home and longs for the comforts and familiarity of the life she left behind in India. The story highlights the stark contrast between the different socio-economic backgrounds of the characters and the impact that this has on their lives.

Another example of class distinction in Divakaruni's work is *The Palace of Illusions.* In this novel, Divakaruni retells the story of the Mahabharata from the perspective of Draupadi, a powerful and influential character in the original epic. Draupadi is born into a royal family and enjoys a life of privilege and luxury. However, when she marries the five Pandava brothers, she finds herself ostracized and marginalized by the rest of the royal court. The novel explores the dynamics of class distinction and the impact that it can have on relationships, both within families and between social classes. In her works, Divakaruni draws attention to the complex interplay between class, race, and gender in the South Asian diaspora and the United States. She highlights the ways in which class distinctions often intersect with other forms of discrimination and marginalization, and the impact that this can have on individuals and their lives. Her works also draw attention to the prevalent stereotypes and assumptions about different social classes, and the need to challenge these biases and misconceptions. Through her characters' experiences, Divakaruni highlights the social hierarchies that exist in the South Asian diaspora and the United States and underscores the need to challenge these inequalities and work towards a more equitable and just society. Divakaruni's writings depict the ways in which women are relegated to secondary roles, facing restrictions and limitations on their opportunities and freedoms, as well as the societal norms and expectations that confine women's choices and perceptions. The theme of gender discrimination permeates Divakaruni's novels and short stories, underscoring the urgent need to challenge and change the patriarchal norms that have long suppressed women's full humanity. In *Sister of My Heart*, the characters Anju and Sudha struggle to assert their independence and pursue their dreams in the face of traditional gender roles imposed by their conservative family. The novel explores the difficult choices and compromises that women face as they strive to balance their responsibilities to their families with their individual desires and aspirations. The story reflects the pervasive gender discrimination evident in Indian society, where women are often expected to follow traditional roles and submit to patriarchal authority.

Another example of gender discrimination can be seen in *Palace of Illusions*. Throughout the novel, Draupadi faces constant discrimination and marginalization, as her decisions and actions are often overridden by her husbands and male members of her family. The novel highlights the deeply ingrained gender bias in Indian mythology and culture and serves as a critique of patriarchal attitudes that relegate women to inferior status. *The Mistress of Spices* explores the experiences of an Indian woman living in Oakland, California, who works as a spice mistress, dispensing remedies and advice to customers. The novel highlights the double burden of gender and race discrimination faced by women of color in the United States. The protagonist Tilo struggles to balance the traditional expectations of Indian society regarding women's roles with the American values of individual freedom and self-determination. The novel also addresses the dilemma of assimilation and the difficulty of reconciling different cultural expectations and values. In *Arranged Marriage*, Divakaruni explores the ways in which gender discrimination can affect women across different generational and cultural contexts. The stories depict women facing issues such as domestic violence, sexual harassment, and lacking autonomy over their own lives. The collection illustrates the insidious ways that gender discrimination can manifest in everyday life, from expectations about women's roles and responsibilities to the ways in which women's concerns are dismissed or trivialized in patriarchal societies. Divakaruni's works depict the pervasive and insidious nature of gender discrimination in Indian and Indian American societies. Her writings often challenge traditional gender roles and expectations and shed light on the ways in which women can assert their independence and pursue their dreams in the face of social barriers at varying degrees. By depicting the lived experiences of women, Divakaruni's works help to highlight the urgency of addressing gender discrimination and challenging patriarchal norms that have long suppressed the full humanity of women.

The theme of widowhood in Divakaruni's works explores the ways in which societal norms and traditions can impact the lives of women who lose their husbands. Her writings illustrate how these women are often marginalized and face many challenges in navigating their new roles, both within their families and within their broader communities. In *The Mistress of Spices*, Divakaruni's protagonist, Tilo, mourns the loss of her husband and is forced to live alone, as family and societal expectations prevent her from remarrying. The novel follows Tilo as she navigates her grief and tries to find purpose in her life as a spice mistress, while still adhering to the constraints of her widowhood. The novel illustrates how traditional beliefs and societal expectations can limit a woman's opportunities for personal growth and development. Similarly, in *Sister of My Heart*, Divakaruni's characters Anju and Sudha face significant challenges in dealing with their widowed mother. The novel explores the ways in which traditional expectations place a heavy burden on women who become widows, and how these women must navigate between the expectations of family and society while also seeking to assert their own agency and independence. Through the characters of Anju and Sudha, Divakaruni highlights the difficulties that widows face in a patriarchal society, including the loss of their economic and social status.

Divakaruni's works also examine the experience of widows in the Indian diaspora community. In "Arranged Marriage," the short story "Doors" explores the challenges faced by a widow who is sent to live in the United States with her daughter-in-law. The story highlights the difficulties of adjusting to a new culture, as well as the isolation and loneliness that can come with being a widow. Additionally, the story illustrates the tensions that can arise between traditional Indian values and Western values, and how these tensions can affect a widow's ability to integrate into a new society. Overall, Divakaruni's works on widowhood shed light on the complex and often painful experiences of women who lose their husbands. Her writings explore the ways in which traditional beliefs and societal expectations can limit a woman's opportunities for personal growth and development, and how these women must navigate between the expectations of family and society while also seeking to assert their own agency and independence. By depicting the challenges and struggles faced by widows, Divakaruni's works serve as a reminder of the importance of supporting and empowering women who face such difficult circumstances.

Divakaruni often explores the theme of domestic violence and its impact on women's lives within the social milieu of South Asian culture in her works. Domestic violence, which includes physical, emotional, and psychological abuse, is pervasive across cultures, and Divakaruni's works shed light on the damaging impact it has on women within the context of their social surroundings. Throughout the story of *The Palace of Illusions*, Draupadi faces physical and emotional abuse from her husbands and the other male characters, highlighting the issue of domestic violence in the context of a patriarchal society. Divakaruni's portrayal of Draupadi offers a critique of how women's power and agency are often constrained by their social roles and the expectations of their husbands and families. In *One Amazing Thing*, Divakaruni portrays domestic violence in a different context, showcasing how it can occur within seemingly ordinary families. In the novel, Uma, a character seeking a visa, is trapped in a consulate building when an earthquake hits. As the group waits for rescue, they begin to share their life stories, and Uma reveals how she suffered abuse from her own husband. Uma's story points to how domestic violence can happen in any context and how it can be deeply damaging to women's psychological well-being. Divakaruni's short stories also explore the theme of domestic violence, such as "Clothes," where the protagonist, Sumita, is trapped in a marriage with an abusive husband. The story explores the issue of domestic violence within a cultural context where divorce is stigmatized, and women are expected to endure abuse for the sake of their family's honor. Overall, Divakaruni's works highlight domestic violence in the context of South Asian culture, emphasizing how it is often overlooked and normalized, and how it can have profoundly damaging effects on women's lives. Her works serve as a call to action, urging readers to recognize and challenge patriarchal structures that enable domestic violence, and to empower victims to speak out against this pervasive issue. Through her writing, Divakaruni helps to raise awareness about domestic violence and serves as a voice for women who have endured its tragic effects.

One of the themes that she delves into is abortion, which is a complex and controversial issue within many cultures. In her writings, Divakaruni explores the topic of abortion in the context of the social, cultural, and religious norms that shape women's experiences. One of her most well-known works that deals with abortion is *Sister of My Heart*. The novel explores the story of two cousins, Anju and Sudha, both growing up in an Indian household. Sudha, who is unmarried and becomes pregnant, decides to have an abortion, even though this goes against the traditional expectations of her culture. The novel showcases the complexity of the decision to have an abortion and the impact on the characters involved. In *Oleander Girl*, Divakaruni explores the topic of abortion in the context of Indian culture and the idea of filial piety. The novel revolves around Korobi, who discovers that her mother was forced to have an abortion due to the family's desire for a male child. The novel highlights the struggle of women in a patriarchal society who are subjected to the pressure of producing a male child. Divakaruni's exploration of abortion also extends to short stories, such as "Mrs. Dutta Writes a Letter," in which an elderly woman reflects on her choices after having an abortion when she was younger. The story illustrates the effects of cultural and societal pressure on women and their choices, as well as the continuing impact these decisions can have on one's life. Overall, Divakaruni's writings on abortion showcase the complexities of the issue, including the cultural, social, and religious factors that affect women's decisions. Her works challenge the notion that women should be forced to adhere to traditional expectations, ultimately highlighting the importance of women's autonomy and agency over their own bodies. Through her writing, Divakaruni encourages readers to consider the impact of societal norms on women's lives and to re- evaluate traditional views on women's reproductive rights.

The theme of divorce is a prominent one in Divakaruni's works, highlighting the impact of societal norms and cultural expectations on the institution of marriage. Her writings depict the struggles and challenges faced by women who choose to leave their marriages or have no choice but to do so. Divakaruni's works portray the complexities of the issue of divorce within the context of social norms, cultural expectations, and societal pressures. One of her most significant works exploring the theme of divorce is *Queen of Dreams*. The novel follows the story of Rakhi, a young woman who has been married for fifteen years and is going through a difficult divorce. The novel moves back and forth between Rakhi's past and present, highlighting the complex emotions and struggles she experiences as she navigates the end of her marriage. Rakhi's decision to seek a divorce is a courageous act, which goes against the traditional expectations placed on women to stay in unhappy marriages. In *Before We Visit the Goddess*, Divakaruni showcases the impact of divorce on family relationships. The novel follows three generations of women who have experienced unexpected and unplanned separations. Sabitri, the grandmother, is separated from her husband when she is a young mother and must raise her daughter as a single mother. Bela, Sabitri's daughter, experiences a difficult divorce herself and is estranged from her daughter. The novel highlights the impact of these separations on how the family relationships are shaped, and how the pain works to solidify or confront these relationships.

Divakaruni's works also portray the societal and cultural expectations that women struggle with when they face the possibility of divorce. In *Oleander Girl*, Divakaruni highlights the stigma associated with divorce in Indian society. Korobi, the protagonist, is engaged to an NRI Indian boy, but her dreams of a happy marriage and a new life in the U.S. are shattered when she discovers a letter from her mother indicating that her parents divorced. The revelation exposes Korobi to the stigma attached to divorce, which is a reflection of society's attitude towards women who choose to leave an unhappy marriage. The theme of divorce is also examined in "Arranged Marriage," where Divakaruni features stories of women who have left their husbands, or been left by them. The stories challenge the societal expectation of a woman's ultimate goal of marriage, highlighting how the institution of marriage is not always the perfect solution for every individual. The stories also showcase the impact divorce has on women's lives and the challenges they face when they try to rebuild their sense of self and independence. Overall, Divakaruni's writings underscore the theme of divorce, highlighting the complexities of leaving a marriage and how societal norms and cultural expectations impact women's choices. Her works bring to light the emotional struggles of women who must navigate the pain of separation and societal stigma. Through her female characters' journeys, Divakaruni showcases the resilience and strength of women who choose not to accept societal expectations, standing up for themselves against the odds.

Divakaruni's works often explore the theme of love and marriage and how they are shaped by social and cultural norms. They depict the struggles of women in patriarchal societies, where marriage is often seen as the ultimate goal for women. Her works deal with the complexities of these relationships, the societal pressure to conform, and the impact of cultural expectations on romantic relationships between men and women. In "Arranged Marriage", a collection of short stories, Divakaruni explores different facets of arranged marriage. The book portrays women's experiences in arranged marriages, highlighting the challenges they face, such as the lack of control, the pressures to conform to gender roles, and the unfulfilled expectations of love and intimacy. The stories also examine the often-unseen power dynamics within married life, where women have limited agency and decisions are often made by the men. In *The Mistress of Spices*, Divakaruni presents a unique perspective on love and romantic relationships. The protagonist, Tilo, is a mistress of spices who possesses magical powers to heal and help people. Tilo has a difficult past and an uncertain future that makes her reluctant to fall in love. However, when she meets Doug, a charming American visitor, she begins to open herself up to the possibility of love. Their relationship is unconventional, with cultural and language barriers, and marked by other societal differences, indicating the universality of these issues. The novel emphasizes the transcendent power of love to overcome boundaries, but also highlights the challenges of such a relationship, including the consequences of societal expectations about gender roles and marriage.

In *The Palace of Illusions*, Divakaruni explores the concept of love within the context of politics, power and social obligations, creating a nuanced and complicated depiction of the relationships between men and women. *Sister of My Heart* explores the ways in which society's attitudes towards marriage can impact relationships. The bond between cousins Anju and Sudha is tested by their different attitudes towards marriage. While Anju struggles with societal expectations to get married, Sudha falls in love and marries outside of her class. Their relationship is strained as the social norms force them to make difficult choices. The book portrays the challenges of protecting romantic relationships outside of social constructs and the impact of societal expectations on familial bonds. Overall, Divakaruni's works explore the theme of love and marriage within the context of social and cultural norms. Her writing portrays the complexity of these relationships, reflecting the ways they are shaped by larger societal constraints. While her writings recognize the difficulties of navigating the constraints imposed by society, they also offer insight into female agency and empowerment when it comes to romantic relationships. Through her complex female characters, Divakaruni's works highlight the less-talked-about complexities of love and marriage in patriarchal societies.

Divakaruni's fiction often takes place in traditional Indian settings, where the role of women is limited to domestic duties and marriage. However, her works serve to illuminate the challenges faced by women in such environments as they often face restrictive cultural norms, limited opportunities for education and employment, and gender-based violence. Her stories often highlight how women navigate these constraints and carve out their own identities.

In *The Mistress of Spices*, Tilo functions as a powerful figure who subverts patriarchal notions of how women ought to be defined solely by their marital status. Her independence and agency have come at the cost of her being subjected to a life of exile from her own social milieu. Divakaruni gives voice to Tilo's perspectives on marriage and love, and portrays her as an individual with a rich emotional life that extends beyond the confines of social conventions. Similarly, in *The Palace of Illusions*, Draupadi is presented as an individual who possesses her own agency and makes decisions that have far-reaching consequences, while being confined by her own social milieu. This makes Draupadi complex figure who is entirely human and aspirational in her ambition to define her own destiny. Divakaruni brings to the fore Draupadi's agency, resilience, and self-worth, qualities that are often overlooked in the epic. *Sister of My Heart* examines themes like the value of a girl child, the importance of education, and how women experience their sexuality. The novel portrays the nuanced relationship between Anju and Sudha as they navigate cultural and familial expectations in their maturing years. The book champions female solidarity and emotional bonds among women from a lower socioeconomic background. Overall, Divakaruni's works offer powerful portrayals of women in social milieus, addressing issues such as patriarchy, the societal pressure to conform, and other oppressive norms. Her works are notable in giving voice to women characters who are flawed and nuanced, rather than being simplistic, static stereotypes. Divakaruni's writing serves as a poignant reminder that women in social milieus can be agents of change for themselves and a feminist society.

CHAPTER SIX

THEME OF CULTURAL DIVERSITY

Chitra Banerjee Divakaruni is a renowned Indian-American author who has gained recognition for portraying cultural disparity within her novels. Her works emphasize the importance of cultural diversity and highlight the impact of globalization on cultural values, portraying the difficulties faced by immigrants who are attempting to adjust to a foreign culture. One aspect of the significance of cultural disparity in Divakaruni's novels is that it allows readers to understand the complexities of cultural identity. With a world that is becoming increasingly globalized, it is no longer uncommon to find individuals who identify with more than one culture. Divakaruni's novels explore the tension and conflict that arise when individuals are unable to reconcile their identities with their cultural heritage. For instance, in *The Mistress of Spices*, Tilo struggles to balance her traditional Indian values with the American culture in which she lives, and her attempts to reconcile the two create a more comprehensive and nuanced understanding of cultural complexity. Furthermore, the portrayal of cultural disparity in Divakaruni's novels powerfully depicts the effects of globalization on cultural values. As cultures collide, it is clear that there are winners and losers, and Divakaruni's work highlights the risks of losing one's cultural values, traditions, and practices. For example, in the novel, *Oleander Girl*, which traverses India and the United States, Korobi is determined to honor her family's customs when it comes to arranged marriage. Her story, however, is a cautionary tale of the erosion of traditional culture as globalization continues to take over, revealing a loss of values that can have far-reaching consequences.

Another significant aspect of the portrayal of cultural disparity in Dvarkaruni's novels is that it prompts readers to engage in cross-cultural dialogue. As readers learn more about the different cultures presented in the novels, an opportunity arises for individuals from different cultures to engage and understand each other more deeply. Divakaruni's work highlights that the exchange of cultural knowledge and understanding provides an opportunity for mutual learning and growth. Finally, the portrayal of cultural disparity in Divakaruni's novels subtly encourages the preservation and celebration of diverse cultural heritages. Divakaruni's work shows that every culture has valuable traditions and practices that should not be lost, and that cultural preservation does not necessitate an unwillingness to embrace change or growth. The novels emphasize that it is possible to integrate or adjust a cultural practice while still preserving the essence of the culture from which it was derived, leading to a more enriched and multi-dimensional human experience. Divakaruni's works powerfully demonstrate the significance of the portrayal of cultural disparity. Her novels emphasize the importance of understanding one's cultural identity and preserving cultural heritage, often leading readers to engage in cross-cultural dialogue. As the world continues to diversify, the understanding and acceptance of cultural differences become increasingly vital, and Divakaruni's works are a timely reminder of this importance.

Divakaruni explores the theme of the clash of Indian and American culture milieu in her works. Her novels, set across different time periods and locations, highlight the tension between these two cultures and offer insights into the consequences of this conflict on individuals and society. In *The Mistress of Spices*, the protagonist, Tilo, an Indian immigrant, struggles to reconcile her Indian upbringing with the American culture she now finds herself in. Tilo, a mystical figure who uses her magical powers to heal people, experiences a conflict between her traditional Indian values and her new American environment. The novel highlights the dichotomy of these cultures, stressing on the effects of navigating through them. It explores the idea of adapting to change while maintaining one's cultural roots, a process that individuals like Tilo have to go through in a new country. In *Sister of My Heart*, Divakaruni depicts the story of two cousins, Anju and Sudha, who grew up in India but have moved to America. Anju, who was born and raised in America, has assimilated into the culture more easily, whereas Sudha, who arrived later in life, is struggling to keep a hold on her Indian traditions, as she is constantly reminded of the differences between the two cultures. The novel accurately portrays the differences in Indian and American culture, highlighting the difficulties of maintaining cultural ties in a foreign environment.

The Palace of Illusions, Divakaruni's retelling of the classic Indian epic, the *Mahabharata*, also reflects on the tension between Indian and American culture. The book takes a feminist approach to the epic and highlights the different challenges of Draupadi, the protagonist, as she navigates her way through a society that values male dominance. The story also captures the differences between Indian and Western culture in terms of gender roles and societal expectations, resulting in a nuanced exploration of culture clash. In the novel, *Oleander Girl*, the central character, Korobi, is an Indian-American who is deeply connected to her Indian roots. She travels to India to retrieve a family treasure and is confronted with the realities of contemporary Indian culture while still attempting to maintain her strong Indian identity. The novel explores how culture clashes can happen even within the same community, bringing to light the challenges of cultural identity in a globalized world. Lastly, One Amazing Thing depicts the stories of nine people trapped in an immigration office following an earthquake in America. The novel explores the perspectives and experiences of Indian immigrants in America, highlighting the cultural differences they face. Through the characters' narratives, it captures the complexities of identity and diaspora, bringing to light the vivid realities of the immigrant experience. Chitra Banerjee Divakaruni's novels highlight the complexities of cultural identity in a globalized world, portraying the clash between Indian and American culture. Her works explore the tension between different cultures, the impact of globalization on cultural values, and the challenges of navigating cross-cultural relationships. These novels provide a literary understanding of the immigrant experience, mapping out a comprehensive portrayal of life in a foreign land. Most importantly, they illuminate the importance of embracing cultural diversity and can help bridge cultural divides between people of different backgrounds.

Divakaruni has explored the theme of gender roles in social contexts extensively in her works. Her novels, set across different time periods and locations, offer nuanced insights into the complexities of gender roles in different socio-cultural contexts. Her female characters often struggle to navigate the societal expectations and restrictions imposed on them based on their gender, while also pushing back against patriarchal power structures. In this paper, we will explore the theme of gender roles in social contexts in Divakaruni's novels and its significance in understanding how gender shapes social relations. In her debut novel, *The Arranged Marriage*,

Divakaruni examines the gendered experience of South Asian immigrant women in the US. The stories depict women who often struggle to reconcile the cultural expectations of their families with the opportunities of their new homes. The women in the stories are expected to follow the traditional gender roles set out by their families and communities, which often limit their freedom and agency. In one of the stories, "The Bats", a woman is forced to give up her love for a man outside of her caste and instead marries a man who later becomes abusive. The stories show how gender roles have been internalized by women, perpetuated through cultural and social institutions, and reproduced through the family structure.

In *The Palace of Illusions*, Divakaruni re-imagines the story of Mahabharata from the point of view of Draupadi, the wife of the Pandavas. Draupadi's character subverts the traditional gender roles of her time and place by engaging in political discussions, challenging patriarchy, and being vocal about her own desires. She refuses to be defined by her gender and instead asserts herself as a human being with agency. The novel illustrates the complexity of gender relations in ancient Indian society and the ways in which gender roles are constructed and reinforced. Divakaruni's novel, *Sister of my Heart*, depicts the relationship between two cousins in Kolkata, India. Anju, who comes from a well-to-do family, is spirited and rebellious, while Sudha, who is from a poorer family, is educated but more conservative. The novel contrasts the restrictions placed on women based on class and gender, illustrating how women are expected to "stay in their place" in a rigid social hierarchy. Despite these challenges, Anju and Sudha navigate their way through their complex societal roles and maintain a strong connection with each other. In *The Mistress of Spices*, Divakaruni explores the role of traditional gender roles in Indian society through the character of Tilo, a mystical figure who uses her magical powers to help her customers. The novel portrays the tension between traditional gender roles and individual desires and the possible consequences of pursuing one's wishes, in the context of Indian immigrants living in the US. Tilo's character rebels against traditional gender roles by stepping out of the boundaries set for women, undermining the normative expectations of society.

Oleander Girl is a novel set in Kolkata, India, which delves into the complexities of gender roles within the context of an elite Bengali family. Korobi, the protagonist, is on a quest to uncover the truth about her family's past, and in the process, she is forced to confront the gendered expectations of her society. The novel explores the impact of patriarchal values on

Korobi's family dynamic and how this dynamic shapes the relationships of the characters. Divakaruni's novels demonstrate how gender roles are constructed and perpetuated across different social contexts. Her female characters navigate the challenges of their societies while challenging patriarchal power structures and asserting their agency as human beings. By examining gender across time and place, Divakaruni offers a nuanced portrayal of the complexity of gender and its relationship with social relations.

Her novels, set across different time periods and locations, offer nuanced insights into the complexities of gender roles in different socio-cultural contexts. Her female characters often struggle to navigate the societal expectations and restrictions imposed on them based on their gender, while also pushing back against patriarchal power structures. In her debut novel, *The Arranged Marriage*, Divakaruni examines the gendered experience of South Asian immigrant women in the US. The stories depict women who often struggle to reconcile the cultural expectations of their families with the opportunities of their new homes. The women in the stories are expected to follow the traditional gender roles set out by their families and communities, which often limit their freedom and agency. In one of the stories, "The Bats", a woman is forced to give up her love for a man outside of her caste and instead marries a man who later becomes abusive. The stories show how gender roles have been internalized by women, perpetuated through cultural and social institutions, and reproduced through the family structure. In *The Palace of Illusions,* Divakaruni re-imagines the story of *Mahabharata* from the point of view of Draupadi, the wife of the Pandavas. Draupadi's character subverts the traditional gender roles of her time and place by engaging in political discussions, challenging patriarchy, and being vocal about her own desires. She refuses to be defined by her gender and instead asserts herself as a human being with agency. The novel illustrates the complexity of gender relations in ancient Indian society and the ways in which gender roles are constructed and reinforced.

Divakaruni's novel, *Sister of my Heart*, depicts the relationship between two cousins in Kolkata, India. Anju, who comes from a well-to-do family, is spirited and rebellious, while Sudha, who is from a poorer family, is educated but more conservative. The novel contrasts the restrictions placed on women based on class and gender, illustrating how women are expected to "stay in their place" in a rigid social hierarchy. Despite these challenges,

Anju and Sudha navigate their way through their complex societal roles and maintain a strong connection with each other. In *The Mistress of Spices*, Divakaruni explores the role of traditional gender roles in Indian society through the character of Tilo, a mystical figure who uses her magical powers to help her customers. The novel portrays the tension between traditional gender roles and individual desires and the possible consequences of pursuing one's wishes, in the context of Indian immigrants living in the US. Tilo's character rebels against traditional gender roles by stepping out of the boundaries set for women, undermining the normative expectations of society. *Oleander Girl* is a novel set in Kolkata, India, which delves into the complexities of gender roles within the context of an elite Bengali family. Korobi, the protagonist, is on a quest to uncover the truth about her family's past, and in the process, she is forced to confront the gendered expectations of her society. The novel explores the impact of patriarchal values on Korobi's family dynamic and how this dynamic shapes the relationships of the characters. Divakaruni's novels demonstrate how gender roles are constructed and perpetuated across different social contexts. Her female characters navigate the challenges of their societies while challenging patriarchal power structures and asserting their agency as human beings. By examining gender across time and place, Divakaruni offers a nuanced portrayal of the complexity of gender and its relationship with social relations.

Divakaruni's whose works often explore the theme of gender roles in various cultural contexts. Her novels explore the complexities and challenges that women face in societal norms that restrict them based on their gender. Through her characters, Divakaruni emphasizes the importance of questioning gender norms and challenging the patriarchal power structures that are embedded in many cultures. This paper will explore the theme of gender roles in cultural contexts in Divakaruni's novels and its implications for understanding women's lives in society. In *The Palace of Illusions*, Divakaruni retells the epic story of Mahabharata from a feminist perspective through the eyes of Draupadi. Draupadi is born in a patriarchal society where women are expected to be submissive and follow the rules set by men. The novel portrays the struggle of a woman who tries to live her life on her own terms and questions the gender roles defined by society. Draupadi's character serves as a symbol of female empowerment, challenging the gender roles that are the foundation of Indian culture. In *Sister of My Heart*, Divakaruni explores the dynamics of gender roles in the context of two cousins, Anju and Sudha. Anju's character is portrayed as a strong-willed woman who wants to pursue her education and career, while Sudha is expected to follow the traditional path of marriage and motherhood. The novel highlights the limitations and expectations that are set on women based on their gender, despite the significant cultural shift towards modernity in India. In *The Mistress of Spices*, Divakaruni depicts the character of Tilo who is a mystical woman with magical powers, and who runs a spice shop in Oakland, California. Tilo defies the traditional gender roles set by Indian society and takes control of her life through her magical powers. The novel portrays the influence that gender roles can have on the lives of women and the importance of challenging these norms.

In *Oleander Girl*, Divakaruni highlights the theme of gender roles in the context of family drama. The novel explores the dynamics of a family whose traditions are challenged when the protagonist, Korobi, discovers her family's hidden secrets. The novel depicts the complexities of gender roles and their impact on family dynamics and relationships, demonstrating how traditional gender roles can oppress women and lead to trauma in their lives. In *Arranged Marriage*, Divakaruni presents a collection of short stories that explore the theme of gender roles in the context of the Indian immigrant experience. The stories depict the struggle of women who are caught between traditional gender roles and the opportunities presented by the new culture they have entered. The women in these stories are confronted with the challenges of reconciling the old and the new, and the tensions that arise when they attempt to assert themselves in a patriarchal society. Divakaruni's works highlight the pervasive nature of gender roles in various cultural contexts and the ways in which they impact the lives of women in different ways. Her novels challenge the traditional gender norms that limit women's freedom and demonstrate the disruptive effect of individual female empowerment on patriarchal power structures. Through her novels, Divakaruni encourages readers to question gender roles and to recognize the role they play in shaping our cultural societies.

Her works delve into the experiences of Indian women who are caught between their cultural traditions and the demands of modern society. In *Arranged Marriage*, Divakaruni presents a collection of short stories that examine the experiences of Indian women who have emigrated to the United States. Throughout the stories, Divakaruni contrasts the traditional expectations of Indian culture with the challenges and opportunities of modern society. In "Meeting Mrinal," for example, a woman who has recently immigrated to the United States struggles to reconcile her traditional values with the new opportunities that are available to her. She must balance her sense of duty to her family with the desire to pursue her own goals and ambitions. In *Sister of My Heart*, Divakaruni examines the theme of cultural disparity through the relationship between two cousins, Anju and Sudha. While Anju is raised in a traditional Indian household, Sudha is raised in a more modern family. The novel explores the cultural differences and challenges that the two women experience, highlighting the differences in their experiences and the struggles that they face as they try to navigate the complexities of their family and society. In *The Mistress of Spices*, Divakaruni explores the theme of cultural disparity in the context of an Indian-American protagonist, Tilo. Tilo is a mysterious woman who runs a spice shop and possesses magical powers. The novel shows the tension that arises in Tilo's life as she attempts to reconcile her traditional Indian values with the demands of her modern American customers. Divakaruni uses Tilo's story to explore the complex experiences of immigrants and their struggle to preserve their cultural identity in the face of assimilation.

In *Oleander Girl*, Divakaruni depicts the dissonance between traditional Indian culture and modernity through the story of Korobi, a young woman who is preparing for an arranged marriage. As she investigates her family's past, Korobi discovers that her family has hidden secrets and that her father is not who she thought he was. The novel explores the conflict between traditional Indian values and modernity, highlighting the challenges that arise when trying to reconcile the two. Throughout her novels, Divakaruni explores the complex relationship between traditional Indian culture and modernity, highlighting the challenges that individuals face as they navigate cultural disparities. Divakaruni shows how the demands of modern society can create dissonance and tension for those who are trying to preserve their cultural identity, while also suggesting that society is dynamic and can transform through the interactions between cultures. Through her works, Divakaruni illuminates the multifaceted nature of Indian culture and society and the complexities of navigating cultural disparities.

Divakaruni is an author who frequently explores the theme of language barriers in her novels. Through her works, she examines the challenges that individuals face when they are living in a culture where they do not speak the language fluently. This paper will examine the theme of language barriers in Chitra Banerjee Divakaruni's novels and the significance of this theme in understanding the immigrant experience. In *Arranged Marriage*,

Divakaruni presents a collection of short stories that explore the experiences of Indian women who have emigrated to the United States. The story "The Word Love" tells the story of an Indian woman who is struggling to learn English. She feels disconnected from her new country due to her lack of language skills and finds it challenging to interact with Americans. The story highlights the isolation and frustration that immigrants can feel when they are unable to communicate effectively. In *The Mistress of Spices*, Divakaruni examines the difficulties that immigrants face when trying to communicate with people who do not speak their language. The central character, Tilo, is a spice seller who has the ability to see into people's souls. Although she speaks English fluently, she struggles to communicate with some of her clients, who speak Spanish or other languages. Through the novel, Divakaruni showcases the challenges of navigating a new culture and language, highlighting the fact that even those who speak the language fluently can struggle to communicate effectively.

In *One Amazing Thing*, Divakaruni tackles the theme of language barriers from a different perspective. The novel takes place in an American consulate in an unnamed Indian city, where the central characters are stuck after an earthquake. The characters, who come from a variety of backgrounds, are all struggling to communicate with one another due to language barriers. However, as they begin to share their personal stories, they find that they can communicate more effectively, and the language barriers begin to break down. The novel highlights the power of communication and the potential for people to connect despite language barriers. In *Oleander Girl*, language barriers are a frequent source of conflict. The protagonist, Korobi, speaks English fluently, but her Bengali family does not. This language barrier causes a great deal of tension in her relationship with her boyfriend, who comes from a high-caste family that has different language traditions. Through this conflict, Divakaruni highlights the role that language can play in cultural identity and the challenges that arise when different languages come into contact. Throughout Divakaruni's novels, language barriers are depicted as a significant challenge for immigrants. The inability to communicate effectively with others can lead to isolation, frustration, and conflict. However, Divakaruni also highlights the potential for individuals to connect despite language barriers. By showing the transformative power of storytelling and the importance of recognizing shared experiences, Divakaruni suggests that language barriers can be overcome. She highlights the isolation and frustration that can come from an inability to communicate effectively with others. However, she also suggests that language barriers can be overcome through shared experiences and effective communication. By depicting the challenges of language barriers, Divakaruni illuminates the complex processes involved in adapting to a new culture and the importance of empathy and understanding in facilitating this process.

Through her works, she explores the experiences of immigrants who encounter numerous challenges, including navigating cultural differences, language barriers, and national identities. In *Arranged Marriage*, Divakaruni presents a collection of short stories that capture the struggles of Indian women who have emigrated to America. In "The Word Love", the protagonist's difficulty in understanding English communicates the challenge of navigating different languages. Similarly, "The Maid Servant's Story" explores the cultural tension between Indian and Western societies, where the protagonist faces discrimination and exploitation due to her immigrant status. Arranged Marriage thus portrays the adjustment issues that immigrants face concerning language, cultural values, and treatment by the majority cultures. In *The Mistress of Spices*, Divakaruni examines the challenges Hispanic immigrants face in America. The novel tells the story of Tilo, an Indian immigrant who is a spice seller in Oakland, California. Tilo has the power to see into people's souls, and she uses her powers to help immigrants who come to her spice shop to heal from cultural dislocation. The novel highlights the challenges of immigrants' lives in the U.S in terms of language barriers, finding work, and adapting to different cultural expectations. Tilo's interactions with her clients offer insights into the complex psychological impact of immigration, cultural adjustment, and the resilience of immigrants in overcoming cultural challenges.

In *Sister of My Heart*, Divakaruni explores the impact of cultural difference on the relationship between two cousins, Anju and Sudha. *Sister of My Heart* depicts the conflict that arises when cultural identities collide, and the characters must navigate cultural expectations while preserving their relationship. The novel highlights the differences between the characters' view of marriage and sexuality, their families' class differences, the alienation of immigrants, and the challenge of adapting to a new country. Overall, the novel captures the tensions that arise from various cultural expectations and traditions that shape individual experiences. In *Oleander Girl*, Divakaruni explores the cultural challenges immigrant families face through the central character, Korobi. Korobi is a young Indian girl who grew up in a traditional Bengali family. Her relationship with her high-caste boyfriend forces her to separate from her society and family's traditions, creating tension between immovable tradition and the liberation offered by modernity. Korobi's experiences showcase the clashes between generations and the impact of conflicting cultural values inherent in a complex set of traditional cultures. Divakaruni's novels emphasize the significance of cultural identity to immigrants and the struggles of navigating cultural differences present in their host countries. The impact of language barriers, racism, class discrimination, and cultural differences is depicted in the lives of immigrant characters. These cultural challenges are a critical part of the immigrant experience, whether in terms of negotiating identities or preserving relationships with loved ones. The stories provide a nuanced understanding of the complex identity struggle that immigrants negotiate in foreign countries and how cultures can begin to come together, ensuring that immigrants are accepted and not continually contentious with the host culture. Cultural challenges faced by immigrants in Chitra Banerjee Divakaruni's novels represent a significant part of the immigrant experience. These challenges deal with language, discrimination, cultural conflict, and reconciling identity. By portraying these challenges through fictional charact

Her novels explore the theme of cultural assimilation through the experiences of characters who negotiate their identity, relationships, and sense of self in the context of diverse cultural worlds. Her works offer a nuanced portrayal of the challenges, opportunities, and complexities of cultural assimilation that people encounter in their journeys of identity formation. One of the earliest works in which Divakaruni addresses the theme of cultural assimilation is *Arranged Marriage*, a collection of short stories. The stories feature Indian women who have migrated to America and who experience alienation and long for a sense of belonging. In "The Bats", a woman named Tara is shown trying to adjust to life in America after marrying an American man. However, she finds herself struggling to adapt to the new culture while maintaining her traditional Indian identity. Similarly, in "Clothes", the protagonist Sumita experiences a sense of disconnect between her traditional Indian culture and the modern American lifestyle, forcing her to confront the difficult questions of cultural identity and assimilation. The collection powerfully portrays the consequences of the interplay between cultures and the struggle of the individual to balance between the competing demands of two culture identities.

In *Sister of My Heart*, Divakaruni explores the complexities of cultural assimilation through the characters of Sudha and Anju, two girls brought up in a traditional Indian culture. As they become adults, each of them encounters different difficulties as they adapt to the American environment where they both live. Sudha finds it difficult to adjust to the American way of life and struggles with her self-confidence, while Anju strives to align her Indian heritage with her American life. The novel portrays the conflict that arises when cultural identities collide and the impact this has on personal relationships. In *Oleander Girl*, a novel set in India, Chitra Banerjee Divakaruni examines cultural assimilation from the perspective of Korobi, the protagonist who moves from a small Bengali town to Kolkata. Korobi's journey of assimilation is initiated when she falls in love with a man from a different Indian caste and later has to navigate the impact of his social identity on her familial ties and ethical obligations. The novel highlights the challenges of adapting to new cultures, negotiating relationships, and the conflict between individual desire and cultural expectation. The theme of cultural assimilation in Divakaruni's novels is significant because it reflects the complex and multifaceted identities and challenges that diasporic and immigrant communities face. The process of assimilation highlights how people struggle to balance their existing cultural expectations and individual identities while adapting to a new cultural context. It highlights the individual's experience of cultural adjustment, dislocation, transformation and the emotional toll it can take. Assimilation is shown to be a dynamic and ongoing process shaped mainly by external and internal forces that lead to the realization that one's cultural identity can never be completely abandoned or accepted. Divakaruni's novels and stories chart the struggles, contradictions and complexities of navigating cultural assimilation and incorporating it into the individual's sense of identity. Her works highlight the larger human experience of migration and transformation, and the importance of understanding where individuals derive their identity from, the demands of the larger cultural system, and how to integrate and balance these identities into a cohesive sense of self.

Divakaruni's works explore the theme of identity question through various lenses, including cultural, gender, and individual identity. Her novels feature characters who struggle to understand their identity and navigate their relationships with others based on their unique self-conceptions. In *Arranged Marriage*, a collection of short stories, Divakaruni explores the identity question of Indian women living in America. The stories portray women who struggle to reconcile their Indian heritage with their American identity. The stories highlight the conflict between cultural expectations and individual desires with a sense of displacement and longing for a sense of belonging. The theme is significant because it underlines the psychological and emotional toll of navigating one's identity when one's roots, cultural traditions, and societal expectations collide with the individual's personality. In *Sister of My Heart*, Divakaruni depicts the struggles of two Indian women, Sudha and Anju, who grew up together and who, as they mature, question their individual identities in the context of Indian society's expectations. The novel highlights the challenges of negotiating sisterhood, gender, and family within a traditional Indian cultural framework. The theme of identity question in this novel is significant because it highlights the inner world of women struggling to understand their roles, value and self-conception; and their attempts to reconcile their individual desires with the responsibilities and obligations stemming from their place in society.

In *The Mistress of Spices*, Divakaruni examines the identity question from the perspective of an expat Indian woman, Tilo, who uses her mystical powers as a spice mistress to help immigrants and others in San Francisco's Bay Area. The novel portrays the struggles of Tilo to reconcile her past with her present and her mystical powers with her longing for human connection. The theme of identity question is significant here as Tilo seeks to uncover her sense of self by navigating her identity through mystical and practical means, all to understand and confront the universal human question of what makes a person who they are. In *Oleander Girl*, Divakaruni explores identity question within the Indian context of caste and privilege. The protagonist, Korobi, is an upper-caste Bengali woman who falls in love with a lower-caste man, Rajat, who lives in the US. The novel features the theme of identity question in the context of family, social class, and cultural expectations, highlighting the tension between individual desire and the societal and familial obligations. The theme is significant because it underscores the complexities of identity, the influences from family, acculturation and environment which affect the understanding of one's true Self. The theme of identity question is an integral part of Chitra Banerjee Divakaruni's works, showcasing the struggles of individuals trying to understand themselves and their identity in the face of cultural expectations, social norms, values, and personal desires. The theme underscores the inner worlds of individuals, especially those caught in between two different cultural worlds, and highlights how the search for identity is continuous, complex, and experiential. Ultimately, the theme offers readers valuable insight into the process and struggles of self-discovery in the face of the ever-shifting relationships and contexts that people encounter throughout their lives.

The novels of Divakaruni explore the theme of cultural disparity, particularly in the context of the Indian-American experience. Her works delve into the challenges faced by individuals and communities trying to reconcile the disparate cultural values and expectations that come with living in two vastly different societies. In *Mistress of Spices*, the protagonist Tilo is an immigrant from India who has been appointed the title of 'Mistress of Spices,' giving her mystical powers to influence people's lives. She struggles to navigate the cultural differences between the Indian and American societies and grapples with issues of identity, belonging, and cultural assimilation. The novel showcases the challenges faced by immigrants in adapting to American culture while preserving their Indian identity. The theme of cultural disparity in the novel is highlighted through the character of Haroun, who is Tilo's love interest. Haroun is portrayed as an American-born Muslim who is conflicted about his cultural identity. He is disconnected from his faith and culture, which he views as archaic and restrictive, leading him to embrace an American identity. This clash of cultures is portrayed through the relationship between Tilo and Haroun, who struggle to reconcile their cultural identities.

In *The Palace of Illusions*, Divakaruni examines the cultural disparity between the traditional Indian society and modernity. The novel retells the epic *Mahabharata* from the perspective of Draupadi, the wife of the Pandavas. Draupadi is portrayed as a strong-willed and independent woman who defies the traditional gender roles of Indian society. Her struggle for independence is undercut by the restrictions imposed on her by her culture and societal expectations. The theme of cultural disparity in the novel is showcased through Draupadi's relationship with her husband, the Pandavas. The Pandavas are depicted as being bound by tradition and societal expectations, leading them to undermine Draupadi's agency and desire for self-determination. The novel highlights the tension between cultural tradition and modernity, illustrating the difficulties of reconciling different cultural values. The significance of the theme of cultural disparity in

Divakaruni's novels lies in its examination of the challenges faced by individuals from different cultural backgrounds trying to adapt to new societies. The novels illustrate the difficulties of maintaining cultural identity while trying to assimilate into a new culture. Furthermore, the novels examine the impact of cultural disparity on relationships, particularly between individuals with differing cultural backgrounds. Divakaruni explores the theme of cultural disparity through the Indian-American experience. The novels tackle the challenges faced by individuals trying to reconcile disparate cultural values and expectations, highlighting the difficulties of maintaining cultural identity while adapting to new societies. The theme is significant in that it showcases the impact of cultural disparity on relationships and the tension between traditional cultural values and modernity. The novels' exploration of cultural disparity provides insight into the challenges faced by immigrants trying to navigate the complexities of a new society while preserving their cultural identity.

Bibliography

- Chakraborty, Banani. "9/11 and the Terror Fear in the Diasporic Community: The Recent Fiction of Chitra Divakaruni". *Fiction of Chitra Banerjee Divakaruni*. 181-193.
- Chaskar, Ashok. Chitra Banerjee Divakaruni's *The Vine of Desire*: A Study of Immigrant's Cultural Dilemmas and Displacements. *Contemporary Discourse*, 5 January 2014. 104-109.
- Xu, Wenying. Reading Feminine Mysticism in Chitra Banerjee Divakaruni's *Queen of Dreams. South Asian Review* 31. 1; November 2010. 186-207.
- Kulkarni, Ashalata. (2012), Gender and Postcolooniality in Chitra Banerjee Divakaruni's *The Palace of Illusions, The Quest* 26 (1) pp. 186-207.
- Deivanai, Valli P. (2011), Self- Revelation in Chitra Banerjee's *The Mistress of Spices. Voices of the Displaced: Indian Immigrant Writers in America.* pp. 163-168.
- Bharati, C. (2013), The Portrayal of Sister – friend in Chitra Banerjee Divakaruni's *Sister of My Heart, The Quest,* Vol. 27, No.2. pp. 61-70.
- Kaur, Raminderpal. (2016), Female's Quest for Identity by Chitra Banerjee Divakaruni with special reference to *Oleander Girl, Comtemporary,* Vol.11 (13).
- Hand, Felicity. (2004), "The Old Rules Aren't Always Right": An Analysis of Four Short Stories by Chitra Banerjee Divakaruni, *The Atlantic Literary Review*, Vol.5, No.3. pp. 61-77.
- Sailaja, P.V.L. and Ramakrishna N. (2011), Travelling across time: A Critical Analysis of *The Mirror of Fire* and *Dreaming and Shadowland, The Quest*. Pp. 20-26.
- Tiwari, Apara. (2013), Trauma and Repercussion in Golding's *Lord of the Flies* and Divakaruni's *One Amazing Thing, Literary Insight*, Vol.4. pp. 114-118.
- http://shodhganga.inflibnet.ac.in/handle/10603/133288
- http:// shodhganga.inflibnet.ac.in/handle/10603/135383